LOOKING FOR IDEAS TO ENRICH AND
ENLIVEN YOUR CLASSROOM SESSIONS?

TURNABOUT TEACHING is the resource book
for you. In the following pages you'll find
the how-to of
  • roleplay, play-acting and mime
  • creative writing as lesson carry-over
  • discussion that's more than just talk
  • art response to Biblical ideas
  • games that really teach

**BONUS: COMPLETE ROLEPLAY SIMULATION
GAME INSIDE**

Turnabout Teaching

Marlene D. LeFever

David C. Cook Publishing Co.
850 NORTH GROVE AVENUE • ELGIN, IL 60120
In Canada: David C. Cook Publishing (Canada) Ltd., Weston, Ontario M9L 1T4

For Naomi Ruth Lefever

My mother and most creative teacher

CONTENTS

1 **ROLEPLAY**
Action lessons that can change lives   11

2 **READ A PLAY**
Bring a new experience to the classroom   29

3 **MIME A MESSAGE**
Put your emphasis on action   38

4 **DISCUSSION**
A lot more than just talk   52

5 **GAMES**
Lead your class in a roleplay simulation   73

6 **CREATIVE WRITING**
Pencil plus paper equals results   111

7 **ART PROJECTS**
Lessons your students can make   138

Foreword

SUNDAY SCHOOL SESSIONS should be times of training when teens and adults learn how to apply what they are studying about God to their life situations. They should feel challenged, excited about the relevance of what they are learning. Some will be discovering their need for a Savior, while many others will be coming to a greater understanding of what it means to live with Christ as Lord of their lives.

When a teacher includes creative methods as an integral part of the lesson, he can direct his students closer to this ideal. Methods never take the place of Biblical content. Rather, methods help students clarify and use the Biblical principles they have studied.

For example: a student emphasizes the value of the Christian life for both himself and his classmates when he uses motions to mime the futility of life without Christ and the purpose of life with Him. Or by playing a roleplay simulation game, students demonstrate how Christians handle emotions like frustration or failure.

In *Turnabout Teaching* you will find step-by-step instructions on how to use each method in junior high, senior high, and adult Sunday school classes (methods can also be adapted for use at special programs, youth groups, and class parties).

Examples of each method are included to give you everything you need to put the method to immediate use.

Turnabout Teaching also gives suggestions for ways students can share what they have learned with others outside the classroom. For example, after students have studied about God's love, they may want to write and present a Scriptural choral reading and slide presentation for another class or the entire congregation.

Be creative! Experiment with the ideas you find here, and develop original ones that emphasize Bible truths and deal with special needs your students have.

Depend on the Holy Spirit's guidance as you use discussion, creative writing, roleplays, and many other methods with your students. Only He can turn people around and get them excited about living and communicating the Christian message.

—Marlene D. LeFever

1

ROLEPLAY

Action lessons that can change lives...

The primary aim of the Christian teacher should not be to cram knowledge into students' heads, but rather to help students apply and use what they are learning. No teaching method has greater potential for helping the teacher reach this aim than roleplay.

Consider the advantages of using roleplay in the classroom.

• *Roleplay stimulates inductive learning.* Most Sunday school students believe in theory that God's Word supplies answers. In roleplay they must find those answers and use them in classroom situations. These practice sessions often make it easier for students to carry what they have learned into their own lives.

Examine what might happen to teens who participate in the following roleplay. The teacher's aim is to help his students discover how to exercise Christian friendship in difficult situations.

Situation: William is obnoxious and rude, so naturally students rarely include him in their activities. John begins to see that his rejection of William is unchristian and decides to ask William to join the youth group's basketball team. He shares his decision with two Christian friends.

Roleplay the conversation among the three boys. Assume that Friend 1 rejects the idea of making friends with William and including him in their activ-

11

ities. Friend 2 begins to see John's point.

In the classroom, the teens would assume their roles:

FRIEND 1: You're crazy if you ask William to play with us. He can't get along with anyone. He'll ruin the team spirit.

FRIEND 2: No, wait. Maybe John's right. Christ would probably let William play.

JOHN: That's my point. If we're going to be Christians, we have to follow Christ even when it's inconvenient.

FRIEND 1: Maybe you do, but I'm not interested. You make the choice. Either you're friends with creeps or you're friends with me.

JOHN: I want to be your friend. I really like you, but I don't want to let Jesus down. I love Him.

FRIEND 2: If you invite William, I'll try to make him feel welcome.

After the three boys have carried the roleplay as far as they can, their teacher would cut the action and begin class discussion. It could go something like this:

TEACHER: Steven, how did you feel playing the part of the Christian who was unwilling to be friends with William?

STEVEN: Cruel. I hope I wouldn't act like that in real life.

CLASS MEMBER: I've got a problem something like this in my school gym class. There's one kid who always gets picked last for teams. He's a wipe out at everything. Maybe the next time I'm captain, I should pick him first.

TEACHER: Even if your choice angered others you chose to be on your team?

CLASS MEMBER: Maybe, if I were convinced I had done what Christ wanted.

• *By using roleplay the teacher achieves nearly 100 percent participation.* Those students who are not actively involved participate by giving their attention to their peers' presentation and by taking part in the discussion that should follow every roleplay.

Participation in learning enhances learning itself.

• *By evaluating what students say in their roleplays,*

12

the teacher is able to determine where his students are and concentrate his teaching in the areas of their greatest need.

• *Roleplay demonstrates to students that from a human perspective everything won't always turn out perfectly for the Christian.* There will be people who won't like them; their witness may be rejected; they may face problems which will never be resolved. Roleplay can prepare them to handle these difficulties without becoming discouraged or doubting that God cares.

• *Through roleplay and the discussion that follows it, students may find answers to their problems.*

Too often older teens and adults repress their true feelings during the Sunday school hour. Even though they might want help or clarification, they may be ashamed or afraid to ask for it. But in a roleplay, they assume identities of imaginary people. Through these people, players are able to vocalize their own negative or divergent attitudes in the security of a play situation. As the class deals with "imaginary" problems, it can help students who are facing the same or similar difficulties in real life.

Consider the adult who feels bitter toward God and other people. Perhaps he refused to take part in a shady business deal and consequently went bankrupt. What insights might he gain from the following roleplay, even if he only participated by listening?

> *Situation: Joseph has been unjustly accused and thrown into prison.*
>
> *Roleplay the debate that might have taken place in Joseph's mind during those years in jail. One student will play Joseph's doubting self, and another, Joseph's trusting self.*

The roleplay might begin like this:

DOUBTING SELF: But, God, I followed You. Is this the way You reward me? I don't understand.

TRUSTING SELF: No, I don't understand, but I remember hearing the stories of how You led Abraham through difficulties. Surely You will do the same for me.

13

• *When students place themselves in the roles of other people, they learn to identify with them, and in this way, they gain significant information about why others behave the way they do.*

Role reversal demonstrates this advantage. Suppose a roleplay in an adult class is dealing with family communication problems. A man and woman roleplay why each feels the communication problem is not his or her fault. About halfway through their play, the teacher asks each to switch roles. The man must continue the woman's arguments while the woman continues his.

When students gain increased understanding of themselves and others, they have paved the way for a behavioral change.

• *There is the possibility that participating in roleplays can help students use their intellectual potential more fully in other areas.* Poor interpersonal relations or feelings of low self-esteem can affect students' intellectual growth. If through roleplaying they come to understand their own and others' behavior better, it could lead to higher all-around intellectual performance.

STEPS TOWARD SUCCESSFUL ROLEPLAY

1. Establish a classroom climate in which adults and teens feel secure. They must know that their ideas and feelings will be respected by you and other students.

2. Be enthusiastic about roleplaying. This necessitates being at ease with the method. You may find it helpful to practice your roleplay before class with a few other people—perhaps family or teachers.

3. As with any new method, be prepared for an imperfect first experience.

The first week Mr. Dye tried roleplay in his teen class, the two students he had chosen stood in front of the group looking helpless.

"I can't think of anything to say," one girl said. "I don't know what to do."

"I can understand," Mr. Dye sympathized. "Why don't I play the part of the girl who has been shoplifting?

14

You play the Christian friend who has seen me break God's rule. That way we can help each other keep the conversation going."

A few students giggled when their male teacher took the role of a thief and a girl, but they soon forgot personalities as they listened to their classmate use principles and verses she had learned to witness to the thief.

You may find it helpful the first Sunday you use roleplay to select a few gifted students before class and go over the play with them. This will assure a successful first experience with roleplay. But after the class is familiar with the method, discontinue these practice sessions. They hinder the spontaneity which is so valuable a part of this teaching tool.

4. Maintain control over all your students during the roleplay. If you have set a serious atmosphere for learning, most discipline problems will be eliminated. Students should realize that roleplays are learning experiences, not simply entertaining skits.

One teacher explained the value of roleplay to her high school class like this: "The situations we are dealing with are the types you may have in real life. If you learn to handle them, you will be better able to share God's message with your friends. Roleplaying may help you become more effective Christians. This may be God's training ground for all of you, getting you ready for work He has for you."

5. Use roleplay frequently. Through practice students get more proficient and increase the method's teaching value.

6. Encourage as many students as possible to participate in a roleplay. Match the roles to the students' abilities. A shy student may do just fine in a three-or-four-person roleplay, while he may not be able to handle a situation in which he must carry half the responsibility.

Occasionally, there are characters necessary to a roleplay with which no one wishes to be identified—such as a gossiping woman or a cheating, underhanded salesman. During the initial stages of roleplay, this type of role should be avoided completely. Later unfavorable roles should go to people with enough personal security to carry them off.

Or, use "The Chair" technique. If a situation is too emotional or a character too threatening for a student to play without overacting or causing the class to think of him as the type of person in the role, assign that role to "The Chair."

The students in the roleplay would direct all their comments to "The Chair" when they respond to the objectionable person. The teacher, standing in the background, should give the responses he thinks "The Chair" in its assigned role might give. Students would behave toward "The Chair" as if it were a real person.

7. Prepare the class before the roleplay begins for its part in the presentation. Suggest each student identify with or try to experience the feelings of one or more of the characters. Explain that everyone is included in the discussion following the roleplay and that students may be asked to give their feelings about certain responses or suggest alternate ways the roleplay might have been developed.

In difficult roleplays, or when the players do not have a strong Bible background, consider assigning class helpers to each player. These helpers meet with their player before the roleplay begins to decide what position he will take. At points during the roleplay, you may stop the action and allow players to ask advice from class helpers before resuming the play.

Or, as an alternate to the class helper idea, you may want to send an additional student into a roleplay to help a player who is having difficulty. For example, if the "Christian" player is unable to answer the questions of a "non-Christian," you might introduce a second "Christian" to the situation to keep the conversation progressing.

8. Cut the roleplay when:
• the group has seen enough of the situation to analyze the problem and make helpful suggestions.

• the group can project what would happen if the roleplay were continued.

• the players have reached an impasse, and it would serve little purpose to send in additional students to prolong the play.

• there is a natural closing.

9. Always follow up the roleplay with a discussion of what happened during the roleplay itself. This will include questions such as: what do you think each character was feeling? Why did he react the way he did?

10. Lead the students from the discussion of the roleplay into a personal application of what they learned from the experience. Questions such as, "Why do you think that character acted the way he did?" might change to "What makes us act like that sometimes?" This application is actually an inductive guide designed to help learners transfer what they learned in the classroom roleplay to their own life situations.

Also as part of this final step, the students might suggest ways they could improve the roleplaying technique and give suggestions of other problem areas with which they would like to deal through roleplay.

To summarize the entire roleplaying process: first the teacher presents the situation and instructs his students so they will be able to get the maximum benefit from it. Second, the dramatic action is presented. And finally, there is the application. Not one of these steps may be excluded if the roleplay is to be completely effective.

NOW IT'S TIME TO ROLEPLAY

Study the following situations. Each can be used to help introduce your class to roleplaying. Read or tell the situation to your class. Then follow the directions at the end of each roleplay.

The first, "How to Ditch a Friend," is designed for junior high and senior high girls. It is especially effective when it is used in lessons that center around living the Christian life.

How to Ditch a Friend

The Group had been "The Group" ever since school began. It was unofficially composed of the prettiest girls in the class. Girls from this clique always got elected to class offices. They laughed a lot and seemed to enjoy life more than any of the girls who weren't a part of The Group.

From the beginning of the year, Cory had made up her mind that she would break into The Group, even though she thought it might mean seeing less of Lois.

Lois was her best friend. They could share their thoughts and special secrets. Often they planned their devotions together. But Lois was dumpy-looking, and somehow her clothes always seemed out of date. The Group would never accept Lois.

So Cory began her infiltration plan. She started sitting at the same lunch table with The Group. And when her mother asked who she wanted invited to her birthday party, she mentioned only the names of the girls in The Group and the fellows they talked about.

The Monday after the party, Cory was talking to Lois when Sandy, a girl from The Group, walked by. "That was a great party, Cory," she said. "I'll save you a seat in the cafeteria this noon."

Sandy walked away without saying a word to Lois. It was just as though she hadn't seen her at all.

Roleplay. Roleplay the conversation Cory and Lois might have immediately following this incident. How does Cory explain the party and how does Lois react? Each girl should try to honestly share with the other how she feels in such a way that their friendship will not be permanently damaged. Each girl should learn something about herself and about friendship through the conversation.

Roleplay. Roleplay the conversation between Cory and Sandy as Cory explains the importance of her friendship with Lois. Cory might attempt in this conversation to break down the clique she has tried so hard to join.

Note that "How to Ditch a Friend" leads students to a crisis point. At that point, participants should have little trouble reacting to the situation. And because the problem itself is specific and not too complex, students will be able to solve it successfully.

Nearly every girl will identify with at least one character in this roleplay. This identification will make it easy for her to participate in a discussion following the roleplay.

Opening discussion should center on the roleplay itself.

1. How do you think Cory felt about herself throughout this roleplay?

2. If Cory had to choose between her friendship with Lois and her friendship with Sandy, which do you think she would choose? Defend your answer.

Then help the students personally apply what they have learned through the roleplay by asking questions like these:

1. Why is it so easy for Christian teens to form cliques? What could our class do to help dissolve existing cliques and keep others from forming?

2. How do you think Christ might finish the following sentence? One of the qualities I would like to find in Christian friendships is _____, because _____.

During the discussion, the teacher acts as a guide, asking questions, listening to comments students make, usually keeping the students on the lesson topic.

Occasionally, however, a student will ask a question or make a comment that the teacher knows will change the lesson's focus. For example, suppose that during the discussion of the above roleplay, a girl would say, "What's wrong with being popular? As far as I can see, Sandy wasn't the villain here. Why are Christians always against success?"

The teacher should evaluate the question—in this case, what is the Christian's view of success? If he feels the student genuinely wants an answer, he should allow the discussion to switch directions. Real needs of students and their questions should take precedence over lesson plans.

The roleplay, "Home Is Hate," is designed for junior high, senior high, and adult students. It should be used in lessons that center around witnessing and living the Christian life.

Home Is Hate

About three months ago this same time of night, Tor had sneaked out the back door determined never to return home again. Now he stared at that door, waiting for courage to knock.

He could almost hear the fights and the sobbing, and see the hypocritical pecks on the cheeks when others were watching—his parents, and the life he'd run from.

Tor often wondered what kept them together. He'd even hoped for divorce so the bickering and pretence would end.

Then that night for no specific reason, no big fight, he had just reached his end. He couldn't live in that house anymore.

"Why come back?" he reasoned. "After the welcoming scene, everything will be the same. The walls will close in on me again."

But he'd promised God he'd chance it, so he had to knock.

Through Kurt, a guy he'd met on a beach, Tor had discovered Jesus Christ. He'd been accepted at a Christian hostel and, for a perfect month, he had learned about his new God.

Then last week at dinner, Kurt said, "Tor, don't you think you ought to go home and tell your folks what's happened?"

"My home is hate," he answered. Then with vivid illustrations, he shared his parents with the group. He wanted to convince them it would be wrong to return, but by the time he finished talking, he knew what God expected of him regardless of circumstances.

Now back home, he prayed a final time, "I wish You

hadn't asked, Lord." He knocked. Seconds later a light went on upstairs.

Roleplay the conversation that takes place between Tor and his parents. Try to capture the feelings each might have. Develop the questions the parents would have about Tor's running and Tor's explanation. Include how Tor would give his testimony and the reactions the parents might have to his newfound faith.

Roleplay for adults. Roleplay the conversation between Tor's parents after Tor goes to bed. Assume that, in spite of Tor's witness, their attitudes remain the same. Then replay the conversation assuming that their attitudes are beginning to change, and they are evaluating their relationship with each other and God.

In roleplays like "Home Is Hate" in which emotions play a large part, the teacher may want to stop the conversation at an emotionally charged point and ask each player to remain in character while he soliloquizes on how he feels at that moment. By reflecting out loud, the actor is better able to evaluate his responses, and this additional data helps the other players and the audience participate more completely in the roleplay.

Discussion questions on a teen level for this roleplay might include:

1. Suppose the same pressures Tor ran away from build again. Now that he is a Christian, how might he handle them?

2. In what ways other than through his spoken testimony might Tor witness to his parents?

On the adult level, a discussion leader might ask: how might these parents work to build a new relationship between themselves and with their son?

The purpose of the lesson will determine the type of application questions that would be most effective here. If the purpose is to train teens to witness to those around them, an application question might be: why is it often harder to witness to those we know than it is to tell strangers about Christ?

21

But if the adult class is studying interpersonal relationships, they would gain more from a question like this: if you could share with a new Christian just one principle on successful Christian family living, what would it be?

The next roleplay, "Small, Round Compact," was designed for senior high and some junior high students. You may want to assign the part of Julia to "The Chair." Assign the roles to the players before the situation is read.

Small, Round Compact

Charlene sat stiffly on the edge of the bed and stared at her bulletin board. It displayed all the treasures of her senior year—Stu's rose, a picture of a blond holding gas-filled balloons, the cover of "TIME" which was a collage of things associated with women. She had used that cover to illustrate her women's lib paper for social problems class. Then it had meant an A, but now the little, round compact in the corner of the collage seemed to fill the room.

In her hand she held an identical birth-control compact she had found in her 15-year-old sister's drawer.

"Julia's sleeping with John!" Charlene said out loud as if the connection of the case with real life just hit her. "How could You let her do it, God?

"I wish I'd never gone looking for her green scarf," she thought. "Now what am I supposed to do?"

Soliloquy. Charlene should share how she is feeling right now about herself and her role as older sister to Julia. She might include some of the fears she has about confronting her sister.

Roleplay. Roleplay Charlene and Julia's conversation. How might Charlene show her kid sister she is ruining God's plans for her life? What reasons, now that there is little danger of pregnancy, could Charlene give for saving sex for marriage? How might Julia counter her arguments?

Class discussion could be started with questions such

22

as: "How would you answer Charlene's question to God, 'How could You let her do it, God?' " "If you had played Charlene, what additional things would you have said to Julia?" A question such as "What happens when we knowingly go against God's plans?" would guide the students toward personal evaluation.

Some roleplays are designed primarily to develop students' skills. For example, roleplay is one of the most effective ways of training students to share their witness with others. Short problem situations force students to put the information they have learned to use.

Witness Roleplay: Roleplay the conversation you might have with a man who told you he didn't want to hear about your God because teens who attended your church deliberately destroyed some shrubs on his lawn.

Witness Roleplay: Roleplay how you would share Christ's salvation story with a friend who has just told you that his father has cancer and the doctor has diagnosed it as terminal.

Witness Roleplay: Roleplay what you would tell your teacher if he said, "I know you had an oppor-tunity to look at the answer sheet I accidentally left on my desk. But you didn't. Why?"

Witness Roleplay: Roleplay your conversation with someone who wonders how you, in this scientific age, could believe anything so ridiculous as the resurrection of Christ from the dead.

Begin your discussion with a question like this one: "If you had been playing the non-Christian in this roleplay what would your reaction to the Christian's testimony have been? Explain your answer."

The type of application questions you use will depend on your students' involvement with witnessing. If they are just beginning to understand their responsibility, you might ask, "What are some of the things that keep us from witnessing? How can we eliminate these problems?" Or, if many of the class members are already involved in sharing Christ, you could ask, "What opportunities have you had to witness recently? What problems, if any, did you encounter? How did you handle them?"

HOW TO WRITE YOUR OWN ROLEPLAYS

Work alone or in a small group to compile a list of some general problems your class may have. For example:

Junior High	Senior High	Adult
Cliques	Peer pressure	Finances
Scholastic failure	Immorality	Fear of aging
Poor self-image	Fear of future	Prejudice

Then brainstorm possible ways one of these problems could be put into lifelike situations. (Avoid situations which too closely parallel those in which members of your class are involved.) Choose the brainstorm idea that best fits the aim of the lesson you will be teaching. Develop it enough so students will understand the problem when you present it to them, but not so much that you imply a solution. For a roleplay to be a learning experience, the solution must be supplied by the students. Usually it is best to end your prepared situation at a climax point. This forces students to answer the question, "What happens next?" Plan at least one discussion question on the roleplay and one personal evaluation question.

It is unnecessary to write your original roleplays. Simply tell the class about the situation they will complete. This cuts preparation time.

Consider the junior high problem, scholastic failure. You might develop a roleplay like this:

Jon gets poor grades, but he has never cheated in an effort to improve them. His friend Gerry, although he is smarter than Jon, is not as honest.

24

On the day of the unit geography test, Jon prayed, "Please, Lord, help me get a 'C' so I'll pass this marking period."

About midway through the test, he glanced over at Gerry, who was looking at a scrap of paper in his hand and copying something onto his paper.

When the grades came back, Jon had a "D." His friend who had cheated had a "B."

Jon was frustrated, and told a Christian friend how he felt. "I'm not even sure I believe in prayer anymore," he said.

Roleplay the friend and Jon's conversation as the friend tries to help him with his problem by sharing Biblical principles and practical suggestions.

Discussion question: In what ways might the friend's answers be helpful to Jon throughout his life?

Application question: Why is it important for us to discuss questions and doubts we might have about our faith?

An adult teacher may develop a roleplay on the fear of aging.

Mrs. Taylor's whole life has been her children, but now they are grown, married, and living in other cities. "I'm of little use to anyone," she tells a Christian friend. "I really don't know why the Lord doesn't take me home. I'm ready to go."

Roleplay the friend and Mrs. Taylor's conversation in which the friend tries to change Mrs. Taylor's attitude and give her reasons for living.

Discussion question: What do you think was the most important thing Mrs. Taylor learned from this conversation? Explain your answer.

Application question: in what practical ways can we help others find a place in which they can make valuable contributions to others and serve God?

PROJECT CARRYOVER

SLIDE-AND-SOUND ROLEPLAY

Have three or four different groups of students complete the same roleplay. The class should choose the one they consider best. Those chosen should participate in the same roleplay again. This time record both the roleplay situation and the group's solution. Each player should attempt to duplicate the feelings and facial expressions he thinks a person in this situation would have.

A photographer in the class should capture these expressions by taking closeup shots of each player as he roleplays.

Synchronize the slides and tape.

This recorded roleplay can be used in many ways. For example, a slide-and-sound roleplay on prejudice produced by the senior highs could be shown to the whole Sunday school. Then teens could divide the group and guide the different age levels in discussion.

An adult class might record a roleplay for use in the Sunday worship service. For example, a roleplay in which a Christian is an effective witness might be a creative way for a pastor to begin a Sunday sermon on the need for church members to get involved in evangelism.

ROLEPLAY OUTING

Suggest your class plan an outing with another class or church that is also familiar with the principles of roleplay. Ask each person to bring one roleplay situation aimed at the theme for the outing.

For example, the teen and adult classes could use the theme, "Learning About Each Other." The roleplay would deal with areas such as establishing friendships and examining frustrations between the two age groups.

Members of racially different churches might learn from an experimental outing built around the theme, "Let's Get Together."

At the end of the outing each person should share the insights he has gained from this experience. A list of projects that would continue interaction might also grow from this experience.

SHARE A ROLEPLAY

Purchase a looseleaf notebook for your Sunday school library and label it, "Roleplays That Work." Ask each teacher who develops a successful, original roleplay to write it in the book. Follow this format:

Age Level: _____

Topic: _____

(*Roleplay itself written here.*)

Discussion Questions: _____

Application Questions: _____

Created by: _____

Used by: _____

ROLEPLAY A BIBLE STORY

Some young teen classes find roleplaying Bible stories they have studied a valuable experience. When they become involved in the situations, they are better able to understand some of the temptations, triumphs, and challenges Biblical people experienced. This understanding helps teens apply to their own lives the principles these stories illustrate.

One class had an audiovisual tape recorder available to them, so they decided to record the "Life of Joseph" and invite their families to see their movie.

It took three hours one Saturday afternoon to complete the half-hour tape. The students first talked through what they planned to do in each scene. Then they roleplayed each scene approximately the way they wanted to record it on tape. Students who were not involved in that scene would give their opinions about anything they felt was good or in need of change.

In one scene Joseph was in prison. The teen playing the part of Joseph knelt and prayed to God not only to help him but also to give him the strength to be a good witness to others around him. When the scene ended, his classmates didn't crowd around the video set to see the replay the way they usually did. Instead a friend of the player asked, "You were really praying, weren't you? I mean, you weren't just acting?"

The 13-year-old boy answered, "I guess God wants us to do things for real or others who watch this won't see much more than just a story."

The teens invited their parents to see and discuss their finished roleplay. Many came, some who had never been to the church before.

After the film, one father said, "It's not for me. I just can't seem to reach God, but my son has. I hope he never loses what he has found here in church."

2

READ A PLAY

Bring a new experience to the classroom ...

Read a play? Sure, it might be a new experience, but how can it help students grow in their Christian lives?

First, reading plays can force students to look at familiar truths in new ways. The right play in the hands of a creative teacher can be a tremendous teaching tool. Imagine what might happen in a senior high class if on Easter Sunday morning they are not asked to sit through a retelling of Christ's death and resurrection once again. Instead, their teacher gives them each a copy of the play, *Christ in the Concrete City.* As they read aloud the modern verse drama, they find themselves at the foot of Christ's cross, examining the part their sin played in the death of the Lord of the Earth. Christ forgives them, and suddenly many experience in a new way the celebration of Easter. These students are ready to participate, perhaps for the first time, in the joy of the resurrection.

Second, reading plays equalizes everyone's experience. For example, visitors to the class are able to participate in both the presentation and discussion of the play, along with those who may be more familiar with Christian concepts. Also, shy students are able to respond with the same enthusiasm and success as those who are more outgoing. Stage fright, which accompanies memorization (and original-response roleplay), is eliminated.

Finally, reading plays exposes the class to a wider

range of experiences than they could ordinarily have. For example, they can go back in time to the crucifixion or become members of another culture.

Difficult dramas can be read because the production is audience-centered rather than stage-centered. And plays with large casts can be presented since a student can read more than one part.

PICK A PLAY

Evaluate each play you consider by answering the following questions. Any selection that does not get a yes answer on at least the first three questions should not be used.

1. Is the subject matter important enough to be worth the time my class will spend on it?

This involves deciding how your students will benefit from the reading. The amount of class time to be devoted to the drama should also be considered. If your period is just 50 minutes long, it would be unwise to select a 45-minute reading. Much of the drama's value comes from the discussion that follows the presentation. If you cut discussion short, you will be giving your students an entertaining hour, but you will not be training them to apply what they have experienced.

2. Is the play suited to the age level, experience, and needs of my students?

3. Is the plot interesting enough to hold my students' interest throughout the story?

4. Is there a conflict within the story that must be resolved?

A story without conflict may produce an animated lesson, but it is not a play. A good play gets the audience into it immediately, builds to a climax, and completes itself.

5. Are the characters believable to the audience?

This doesn't mean that the characters in all good drama act in predictable ways within situations that are copies of life. One group of contemporary playwrights depict absurd characters in absurd situations. By removing their characters from the real world many are able to comment in a unique way about the problems of humanity. However, within the play, the characters remain consistent, believable.

6. Does the dialogue seem right for the character?

7. Is the action honestly motivated?

If a character gets angry, changes his convictions about something, commits a crime, there has to be a logical reason for this, built into the play.

After you have chosen a play, become thoroughly familiar with it before you introduce it to your class. Read it through several times, and get to know the characters.

As you read, jot down possible discussion questions. For example, if you have chosen T. S. Eliot's *Murder in the Cathedral,* a poetic drama about Thomas a Becket's temptations, sainthood, and martyrdom, you might ask: In what ways are Becket's struggles with temptations similar to struggles we have today?

DON'T RULE OUT SECULAR PLAYS. Consider reading sections from these plays in class. Ask your students to apply Christian principles to the situation or give Christian answers to questions implied by the play.

For example, in Samuel Beckett's tragicomedy, *Waiting for Godot,* two clown-tramps wait for Godot to arrive and give some meaning to their lives. But Godot never comes.

Students might discuss: What gives the Christian's life meaning? Could Beckett have been implying that Godot is God? If so, what should be a Christian's response to a world that can't find God?

GETTING THE CLASS PREPARED

Some preparation is necessary to make reading a play a successful experience for your class. Many people have never developed their voices and interpretative skills. For the reading to come alive, students must express the emotions, attitudes, and actions of their characters by using their faces, voices, and bodies.

The following exercises will take just five minutes of class time each period for three weeks. The first emphasizes expression, and the second, voice quality. On the week before the reading, students will be asked to combine facial expression with hand motions.

If possible, have the class sit in a circle for both the practice sessions and the reading.

Three weeks before the reading: ask each student to say, "Peter is at the door," using the right expression to communicate the attitude you will assign. Assure them that it is difficult to be too expressive. What might sound overdone to the reader is effective to the listener.

(These suggestions are possible reactions to the apostle Peter's escape from prison in Acts 12: 5-16.)

- *Inattention* (I want to get back to the meeting in the living room.)
- *Disbelief* (I thought you were in prison.)
- *Shock and fear* (Maybe it's Peter's ghost.)
- *Excitement* (He's here!)
- *Disgust* (He always shows up and bothers everyone.)
- *Wariness* (Maybe the soldiers have been following him, and he's guided them right to us.)
- *Fury* (Go away and let us pick up our lives where we left off.)

Two weeks before the reading: explain that each person has certain vocal tools. Quality is the sound that is peculiar to him. Loudness, rate, and pitch add variety as he speaks.

Ask students to say, "How about coming to church with me next Sunday," in the way they think it might be said by the character you will assign.

- *An elderly gentleman*
- *An affected society woman*
- *A small child with bubblegum in his mouth*

32

- *A man with a bad cold*
- *A man with a sore throat*
- *A whining woman*
- *A bashful girl*

One week before the reading: acting involves action. When a play is read, most of the action will be facial expressions and hand movements. Ask students to use their faces and hands to reflect the following emotions.

- *A teen who has just decided her date has stood her up*
- *A little boy who realizes that he's brushing his teeth with shaving cream*
- *A woman getting up the nerve to tell her husband she is sorry for getting angry at him*
- *A man changing a diaper*
- *A teen who has just been taken off the team and benched for the rest of the game*
- *A woman trying to build the courage to share her faith with the teen sitting next to her on a bus*
- *A man who just found a fly in his soup*

A student who wants further practice should read children's books aloud. Not only should he put as much expression as possible into his voice, but he should also force his eyes to see several words ahead of what he is speaking. This allows him to occasionally glance up from the page. As he practices, he will be able to see longer and longer phrases. He may find it helpful to run his thumb down the side of the page as he reads so when he looks away from the book, he won't lose his place. This skill gives a student a dramatic advantage when he reads in class, because he is able to briefly establish eye contact with the audience or with another character.

Poor readers may not want to participate in a dramatic reading unless they have practiced before class. Don't hesitate to give out the script. This will not lessen the impact of the group reading. A teacher of teens may even want to schedule a practice reading session with a poor reader.

CREATE A DRAMATIC READING

When a play is not available or when none fits the lesson's needs, it is possible to turn other types of writing into readings. For example, a dramatic reading could be created from a piece of fiction in a Sunday school paper or Christian magazine by cutting such phrases as, "He said," or "She laughed out loud." Then assign the words of the various characters in the story to students to read. Short narration necessary to the plot can be read by one person. Longer sections of narration can be divided among two or more readers.

Occasionally excerpts from newspaper and magazine articles can be worked into readings that draw the students' attention to the Bible lesson. This type of reading has no plot and usually little dialogue. Its impact depends on the way it emphasizes the lesson's message and forces the students to think in new directions.

Consider building a newspaper reading around a theme such as:

Because We Forgot God
He Is My Brother
My Responsibility

For example, in a dramatic reading on the theme, "Because We Forgot God," students might combine articles on political corruption, a hit-and-run accident, and air pollution. Then they could conclude with quotes from the Bible on the alternative life-style Christ offers.

WRITE AN ORIGINAL PLAYLET

Some classes are capable of writing and presenting their own original playlets. Although these are rarely of professional quality, they do have merit. Students participate in the creative process and this gives them enthusiasm and a sense of achievement. Even more important, students learn to share with others the truth they have accepted.

The easiest way to write a playlet is to expand a roleplay. Begin by looking at the lesson in which you want to use the playlet. (Usually allow about three weeks for the creation of the playlet.) Then develop a roleplay that you feel will help your students better understand the message of that lesson.

Now guide your students as they follow these steps:

1. *Become familiar with the roleplay situation.*

If the teen lesson were on salvation, you might write a roleplay like this one, and ask teens to begin their playlet preparation by studying it.

> *Tom admires the Christians he knows and would like to have Christ as his friend too. But when he was in junior high, he introduced his sixth-grade sister to drugs. He was able to stop using them when he realized what they could do to his body, but she wasn't so lucky. She's hooked, and he feels helpless to do anything for her. He feels that he killed his sister's future, and God would never be willing to be friends with him.*

2. *Talk through the problems involved in the roleplay and the different ways those problems might be resolved.*

In the above roleplay, students might discuss what Biblical principles a Christian could share with Tom that would help him understand Christ's love, ways in which Tom might handle the guilt he feels, how a Christian teen and Tom could work together to help Tom's sister.

3. *Decide where the playlet should start, what scenes should be included, how many characters are needed.*

In Tom's story, a conversation between his sister and him would introduce the problems and get the class immediately involved in the situation. This playlet needs only three main characters—Tom, his sister, and a Christian teen.

4. *Roleplay and tape the situation. Then transcribe the tape and edit the transcription into playlet form. Duplicate copies for students who will be participating in the original class playlet.*

The final transcription of Tom's story might begin like this:

Tom: Listen, Cathy, it's bad news. I know, I was almost there. Please stop while you can.

Cathy: Not long ago your story was a lot different. (mimics Tom) "Try this Cathy. Just one pill, Cathy. It will send you into orbit. A new world, Cathy."

Tom: I was wrong.

Cathy: No, you weren't. Why should I give up something I enjoy just because you changed your mind? Now will you give me the money or not?

Tom: No, I can't, Cathy. I feel like I'm paying to kill your future.

Cathy (sarcastically): Let's get super-dramatic about it, Tommy Boy. If you won't lend me the money, I know other ways to get it.

Tom: No! Here's what you need. (*She takes the money and leaves. William enters.*)

William: Say, who's the cute girl? New girl friend?

Tom (sadly): No, my sister. We just had a little argument, and I lost.

William: Better luck next time. Maybe I can cheer you up with an invitation. A bunch of us kids are getting together for a Bible study every Tuesday after school. Since you and I have talked about God several times, I thought you'd like to come.

Tom: If I attended, God would probably strike the whole bunch with lightning. Your God wouldn't want me, William. No way!

This playlet could develop in any number of ways. Cathy could overdose, and William, Tom, and an adult counselor could work with her to help her understand that it is possible to break her habit. She agrees to try and forgives Tom for getting her started. When Tom experiences human forgiveness, he realizes how much greater God's forgiveness must be, and he accepts Christ.

Or, Tom could finally agree to attend the Bible study, and through the teens' witness, accept Christ. That same day, his sister is picked up for stealing a radio and trying to use it to buy drugs. Tom knows he may never be able to undo the damage he's caused in Cathy's life, but he tells her that, if necessary, he will continue praying for her for the rest of his life. Later William tells Tom about a fellow in his neighborhood who has just started popping pills. Suddenly Tom realizes that this could be an opportunity to help someone else in a way he is unable to help his sister. He asks William to introduce them.

PROJECT CARRYOVER

Extend a play's impact beyond your class by reading it to another class, the entire church, or even the community.

Or, the junior high and senior high classes could both develop original playlets on the theme, "How We Could Serve God Better," and present them to each other. In the discussion which would follow, both groups would benefit from the other's ideas.

For these special readings, two or three rehearsals are usually all that are needed.

Readers should sit in a semicircle in the stage area so everyone in the audience will be able to see all participants. The more important characters should be in the middle of the seating arrangement with the supporting players on the outside. Whenever possible readers should sit near those with whom they have the most interaction. This may make it necessary for readers to switch seats from time to time. When those on stage are not in on the action, they could bow their heads and shoulders to show the audience they are not participating in the scene.

Some students enjoy walking through the action of the play as they read. However, for this to be effective, each student must be skilled in the use of eye contact. Otherwise scripts hinder the production.

3

MIME A MESSAGE

Put your emphasis on action...

Mime, derived from the Greek word meaning "to imitate," is dramatic action in which players use motions rather than words to share experiences with the audience.

Many people in this society are embarrassed by a show of emotions, even though it is often necessary and healthy for them to express what they are feeling, and compare and discuss these feelings with others. Mime gives teens and adults a secure vehicle for this comparison and discussion. Because there are no words, students are forced to draw their own conclusions. And as they consider the message of the mime, many will personally apply the truths it demonstrates.

Consider the following mime and how it could be used to teach lessons on friendship.

The Gift of Self

Characters: Everyman
Friend Seeker (FS)

Props: Two paper stars. One star should be pinned to each player.

Everyman sits onstage and mimes reading. He turns the pages, and it is obvious from his expression that he is engrossed in his Book.

FS comes onstage. He seems to be looking for someone. Finally he spots Everyman. He is happy as he goes up to the reading man. He stands there a minute expecting Everyman to notice him. Nothing happens.

He looks a bit puzzled. He walks around Everyman, reaches out and touches him, and finally gives Everyman a terrific shake.

Everyman looks up. He is obviously annoyed at being bothered.

FS mimes a suggestion that they shoot basketball together. Everyman shakes his head no and returns to his Book.

FS walks away, but suddenly he has an idea. He returns. Once again, after much effort, he gets Everyman's attention. Annoyed, Everyman puts his Book on the floor. FS smiles, takes off his star, and with a great flourish, he hands it to Everyman. Everyman looks at it casually, and then his eyes drift down to the floor where he has placed the Book. He resumes reading, and unconsciously, as he reads, he begins to tear the points from the star.

FS is horrified. With every point Everyman tears, FS moves farther away from him. Finally he sinks to the floor and puts his head on his knees.

Everyman finds something important in the Book. He picks it off the floor. With his finger, he underlines what he has just read. He looks embarrassed, ashamed. He sees the torn star on the floor and wipes a tear from his eyes. He sinks to his knees praying. Then he looks around for FS. When he sees him, he goes over and touches him. No response. He tries a second time. Finally FS looks up, but when he sees Everyman, he immediately puts his head down. Everyman tries again. Finally, although he is hesitant and afraid, FS responds. Everyman takes off his star and gives it to FS. FS looks surprised, happy. Everyman helps FS to his feet. Everyman suggests they shoot baskets, and the two walk offstage together.

Like roleplay, mime should not be used without class discussion following it to help students clarify and apply what they have seen. Without this exchange mime is not a complete teaching tool.

Symbols play an important part in most teaching mimes. Begin the discussion by encouraging students to share what they feel each symbol represented.

The following discussion questions would help students analyze what took place in "The Gift of Self."

- What did you feel the star represented?
- What part did the Book play in this mime?
- State what you feel the message of this mime was.

Since there are no words in the mime clarifying exactly what happened, different students may have different opinions. For example, an adult might say, "To me the star represented the gift of personhood. The play told me that unless I give myself to others, my Christianity isn't worth much." A senior high might point out, "The book Everyman was reading had to be the Bible. The mime showed me that reading the Bible isn't enough. Unless we get involved with the world's people, we will never be able to win them to Christ."

PRE-MIME ACTIVITIES

Many students will be unfamiliar with the term "mime," and some may feel inhibited by the process. Explain what it is, and read one example to your class several weeks before you ask students to participate in one. Then follow your explanation with several practice exercises. Use one of the following pre-mime activities each week for two or three weeks before the mime. Choose activities which you can incorporate into your lesson so they actually become part of your teaching plan. If you have time, ask more than one student to complete each activity.

1. (Adult class) Show the three facial expressions you think parents use most often on their children. (Teen classes) Show the three facial expressions you think teens use most often on their parents.

Discuss: How do you think the person on the receiving end of each of these expressions reacts to them? In what ways might they help or hinder your communication with that person?

2. You have just shared your faith with five people, but none of them were ready to accept your Lord. However, all five had different attitudes toward your witness. Use facial expressions to show each of their attitudes. For example, one might be hesitant and another angry.

Discuss: How does knowing a person's attitude help us witness to him? What should be our attitude when people reject our witness? Why?

3. Sometimes we can tell that a person needs our friendship just by the way he walks or sits. First show how a person who is tired and discouraged might walk. Then show how he might sit.

Discuss: What is friendship evangelism? How can we get involved in it?

4. Think of an attribute of God for which you seldom praise Him. For example, His love or His mercy. First tell the class what the attribute is and then pantomime how you would describe that attribute to someone who doesn't speak your language.

A student could pantomime mercy, God's total forgiveness to men even though they don't deserve it, by sinking fearfully to the ground. Hesitantly he glances up and the look of fear changes to one of joy. He raises his hand and slowly rises as if God were lifting him to his feet.

Discuss: Too often we forget to praise God for who He is. How can we incorporate more praise into our class period and into our own devotional lives?

5. Think of three ways you are willing to help God within the church or your community. Pantomime these ways and allow your classmates to identify the service you are demonstrating.

Emphasize that these services do not have to be ones in which the students are already involved, but rather ones in which they are willing to become involved. Use only volunteers for this pre-mime activity, because as they participate, students will be testifying before God and their peers that they are willing to serve Him. This pantomime could lead into a praise and prayer service in which students thank God for the abilities He has given and ask Him for opportunities to put their talents and gifts to use.

Discuss: What are some areas in our church where additional workers are needed? In what ways might members of our class help fill these needs?

6. Divide the class into groups and ask each to pantomime a Bible verse which it feels says something important to their class.

Discuss: What would you tell a new Christian who asks you to explain some methods of Bible study that he might use in his personal devotions?

After the students have been introduced to what mime is and have had an opportunity to participate in several pre-mime activities, they will be ready to put mime to use. Actually, the steps to a successful mime experience in the classroom are much like those of successful roleplay.

STEPS TO SUCCESSFUL MIME

• First examine the mime to make sure it will teach the students something about the lesson they are studying. The mime must carry forth the lesson aim.

• Give students no more than five minutes to prepare for their mime. If they spend too much time practicing, the spontaneity can be lost. During the preparation they should read the mime to get its general ideas. Then they should mime it once before they present it to the group —acting out the script the way they remember it, adding their own touches, and eliminating those which do not blend with their personalities. The script can serve as a jumping-off point. It gives suggestions for actions, but players should be encouraged to add any gestures, expressions, or additions to the story line which they feel would help the audience better understand what is taking place.

The sex of the players is usually of little importance to the mime's story line. Often a character, such as

Everyman in "The Gift of Self," is a microcosm of a larger group of people. Everyman represented all Christians who aren't aware or don't accept their responsibilities to others. Friend Seeker could be anyone, man or woman, who has ever had his offer of friendship rebuffed.

• Prepare the audience for what they will see and later discuss by giving them suggestions about what to look for as they watch the mime. The following general suggestions can help guide students as they watch almost every mime situation.

1. Identify with one of the characters throughout the mime. Ask yourself, "How does he feel? Why does he feel this way?

2. What symbols are being used and what might they represent?

3. What message might this mime have for Christians?

Consider how these suggestions would help viewers understand the following mime, "Masks."

Masks

Characters: three people (A, B, and C)

Props: Three masks. Each player wears a mask made from a paper bag that has been painted black on one side and white on the other. A and B players have the left side painted white and C has the right side painted white. (See Figure 1.) When players face each other, the audience should be able to see only one color.

White A and B face white C and shake his hand (figure 2). Then they all switch places and face the opposite direction so only the black side is showing. The three shake hands again (figure 3). A turns around to face B causing the black and white masks to face each other. A holds out his hand, but B backs away. C comes up behind A and kicks him (figure 4). A falls over. As he turns around to see who kicked him, the black side shows. This pleases C, and he helps

A to his feet and dusts him off. He shakes hands again (figure 5).

B walks over to A and stands facing him. This will put B's white face toward the audience. B places his hand on A's head and pushes down so hard that A is forced to fall in front of him (figure 6). A slowly comes to his feet again and turns away from B so the white side of his face shows. C walks around to face A and B and shakes their hands (see figure 7).

Quickly they change sides again, and black A and B shake hands with black C (see figure 8). All walk offstage.

In "Masks" the discussion might begin with these questions:

1. The racial implications of this mime are obvious because of the black-white coloring of the masks. But what things other than color cause people to have unchristian reactions toward each other and keep them from becoming friends?

2. What types of masks do Christians wear? What can we do first to rid ourselves of masks, and second, to help rid the world of them?

As your students begin to feel at ease with mime, they may want to add musical accompaniment to their performances. Recorded selections must complement the emotional tone of the situation. When a live instrument, such as a guitar, is used, the musician should be familiar with the script so he will be able to anticipate what will happen and accentuate it.

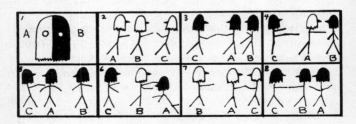

Since there is only one player in the next mime, "The Guilt Bag," and he experiences a wide variety of emotions, it would be an interesting situation to set to music.

The Guilt Bag

Character: Everyman
Prop: Large bag tied at the top with string

Everyman enters the stage, obviously happy, carefree, nonchalant. He pretends to whistle, swings arms, skips.

Then he sees the bag. He stops, examines it closely without touching it. It's obvious that he's impressed.

His attitude turns quickly to one of secrecy. He looks one way and then the other. Slowly, furtively, he reaches out. He grabs the bag and walks quickly away from the spot. He looks tremendously proud of himself, thrilled with what he has taken.

One final time he looks to the right and to the left until he is satisfied that he hasn't been seen. He sits on the floor with the bag in front of him. He reaches out to open it, but as he does, his face suddenly loses its happy glow.

Very slowly and sheepishly, he looks up, frightened. He has remembered that God has seen him. His eyes go from the bag to the ceiling several times. Again his attitude changes. He reaches lovingly for the bag and strokes it. Then he looks up, belligerence and stubbornness showing on his face.

He stands and tries to hide the bag from God with his body, but he finds this an impossible, uncomfortable position to be in.

Suddenly he has an idea. He reaches upward with one hand, but keeps the other hand tightly gripped around the bag. But something is wrong. Evidently he can't find God. He shades his eyes with his hand and scans upward. He shakes his head in sadness because he can't find Him.

Finally, keeping just one finger on the bag, he moves

45

his whole body as far away from it as possible. Again he looks upward, searching. Sad, frustrated, he wipes a tear from his eye.

He looks at the bag one last time. Then with a decisive movement, he jerks his hand from the bag, looks up, and shakes his head yes. He has made his decision to follow God.

His back toward the bag, he lifts his hands toward the sky. He smiles. He hugs himself and clicks his heels together. For the first time since he sighted the bag, he looks happy. Without ever looking at the bag again, he joyfully walks past it and off stage.

Students would find discussion questions like these valuable:

1. What emotions did you feel as you were watching this mime?

2. The bag represents things that separate us from God. What specific sins might the bag represent to Everyman?

3. How did your feelings toward Everyman change during the struggle between his desire for God and his love for the bag?

4. What feelings do you think Everyman was having at the very end of the mime? Have you ever had a similar victory in a struggle with a "bag" in your life? Share how you felt when you finally decided to ask God's forgiveness and follow Him.

• After they have participated in several mimes, your students may want to work with you to construct and act out an original mime.

The group should choose a subject that lends itself to mime—for example, new life in Christ or service to Christ. Students then discuss what situations could be mimed that would help the class understand the lesson better. From these suggestions, they choose the best one and develop it. You may want to use a symbol in your original mime.

Symbols should not be so obscure that their meaning is lost to most of the class. For example, an obvious yet effective symbol to use in a mime about salvation could be tree branches. Those who are satisfied with the old life, life without Christ, could carry dead branches, while those who have made Christ Lord of their lives could exchange their dead branches for ones with leaves.

A group of teens and adults from Circle Church, Chicago, worked for several months on an hour-long original mime they called "Norman Newcreature." In the mime, a modern *Pilgrim's Progress*, Norman struggled with the forces of evil, reacted to interpersonal relationships, and grew in his Christian life. Symbols were obvious and effective. For example, whenever Norman became more interested in the things of the world than he was in spiritual things, he was given a burden (Styrofoam block) to carry. Only through trust in God could he lighten his life's load. The mime made such an impact on the congregation that several other Christian groups in the area heard about it and asked the cast to present "Norman Newcreature" for them.

Usually original mimes need not be written. Students can simply talk through their ideas and practice the action once before they present it to the class.

Idea starter—(*New life in Christ*) Non-Christian Everyman mimes a number of negative activities he is involved in. Then he meets Christ. (What symbol could be used to show the audience that Everyman has accepted the Savior?) Finally he mimes some positive Christian activities that are a part of his new life.

Idea starter—(*Serving Christ*) Use a ladder as a symbol of spiritual growth through service. Everyman climbs a few steps and then comes down and does something for Christ or his fellowman. A second student could play the character "Fellowman." After each service he performs for Christ, he returns to the ladder and climbs a rung or two higher. Occasionally, he might do something to disappoint God and this would cause him to slip back a step.

PROJECT CARRYOVER

The following idea-starter will help you develop a mime and reading presentation in which your entire Sunday school can participate. Consider presenting the finished work to the church on a Sunday when missions are being emphasized.

Title: _____

ASSIGNMENTS

Class Missions Committee: Choose three countries in different parts of the world in which your church supports missionaries, and assign one country to each participating class. Ask the class to develop a pantomime using just three people: (1) a non-Christian national, (2) Scarlet Hat, a person who represents the forces of sin and evil in that country, (3) Blue Hat, a person who represents a witnessing Christian.

In the first part of the pantomime, the non-Christian and Scarlet Hat should illustrate one event in the life of the non-Christian that demonstrates his need for Christ—situations involving stealing, prejudice, hate, etc. If a class were assigned an Asian country, it might develop this pantomime:

> *Asian non-Christian comes onstage. She sits on the floor, and takes off her shoes. Then she steps into the wet rice paddy. She bends almost double as she sticks imaginary plants into the wet soil. She goes across the stage planting row after row, stopping occasionally to wipe her face and rub her back. Scarlet Hat comes onstage and walks quietly to stage right. He is wearing a red hat that has been made by twisting construction paper into a cone shape. He stands with his hands above his head and his legs turned out as if he were an idol.*

48

Asian non-Christian sees the idol and gets a hopeful look on her face. She goes over to it and bows low, praying. Then she gets up and shakes her head sadly. Nothing has happened. She slowly goes back to her rice fields and continues planting one more row. Then both she and Scarlet Hat leave the stage.

In the second part of the pantomime, each class should show what happens when a Christian comes to witness to the non-Christian. Suggest the students be as realistic as possible. Perhaps not every non-Christian will react positively to the message of the Christian. For example, in the Asian situation, part 2 of the mime might go like this:

Asian non-Christian and Scarlet Hat come onstage. Scarlet Hat resumes his idol position on stage right. Asian non-Christian resumes planting in the hot sun. Blue Hat walks on stage. He is wearing a blue cone-shaped hat. He sadly shakes his head when he sees the idol. Then he sees Asian non-Christian planting, and he takes off his shoes and enters the rice paddy. The two of them plant together. As they plant, it is obvious that he is witnessing to her.

Asian non-Christian shakes her head no and runs to the idol. She throws herself in front of it. Blue Hat goes to the opposite corner of the stage and prays. Then he comes back to talk to the woman again. She looks sadly at the idol, and then at Blue Hat. Blue Hat

points toward the sky and smiles. Then he motions for
her to sit beside him. He mimes reading the Bible,
pointing to special passages for her to consider.
Finally Asian non-Christian nods yes, and the two of
them pray together. As they pray, Scarlet Hat looks
disgusted, puts his hands on his hips, and shakes his
head. Finally he sneaks off stage. Asian Christian and
Blue Hat rise and happily leave the stage in the oppo-
site direction from Scarlet Hat.

Briefly summarize what each of the three classes is
planning and give these summaries to the Reader Committee.

Reader Committee: It is your job to coordinate the
program. First study each of the situations you have
been given. Select one or two Bible verses to be read
immediately following the first part of each pantomime.
These verses should deal with man's need for a Savior.

Then prepare a paragraph explaining the message of
salvation to be read after all classes have presented the
first parts of their mimes. Following this reading each
class will continue with the second section of its mime.

Next select short paragraphs from missionary letters
to be read after each witness situation the classes
present. If possible choose letters from the countries in
which the mimes are taking place and select paragraphs
in which the missionaries are praising God for something
He has done. If letters are not available, select one Bible
verse which praises God for salvation, to be read after
each of the three Blue Hat sections.

Choose the best reader from this committee to an-
nounce the names of the countries in which the mimes
are taking place, and to read the message of salvation,
verses, and letters.

Only one complete rehearsal should be necessary since
most of the practice should be done in the individual
classes.

An outline of the program should look something like this:

I. A. Reader: Explain that throughout the presentation, the people wearing the scarlet hats represent the forces of sin and evil while the people wearing the blue hats represent witnessing Christians.
"Now we would like to take you to the country of _____."
Adult class mime (Part I).
Reader's verse on man's sin.

   B. Reader: "Next we go to _____."
Senior High class mime (Part I).
Reader's verses on man's sin.

   C. Reader: "And finally we visit _____"
Junior High class mime (Part I).
Reader's verses on man's sin.

II. Reader presents the message of salvation.

III. A. Reader: "Let's return to _____ to find out what happens when the non-Christian hears about Christ."
Adult class mime (Part II).
Excerpt from missionary letter or praise verse.

   B. Reader: "And now we go to _____ once again."
Senior High class mime (Part II).
Excerpt from missionary letter or praise verse.

   C. Reader: "And finally, back to _____"
Junior High class mime (Part II).
Excerpt from missionary letter or praise verse.

Reader concludes program with prayer that those in your area and around the world who don't know Christ might be given the opportunity to receive Him as Savior, and that Christians will accept their responsibility to share the message of salvation.

4

DISCUSSION

A lot more than just talk...

Discussion is the student-centered activity used most often by Sunday school teachers. And rightfully so. No other teaching method has the class-after-class appeal of discussion.

Students can benefit from discussion in a number of important ways.

First, discussion stimulates interest and thinking, and helps students develop the skills of observation, analysis, and logic.

Second, it helps students clarify and review what they have learned. For example, after an adult class has studied the life of Christ, students might break into small groups to discuss one major emphasis they found in Jesus' teaching and how that emphasis should affect Christians' lives today. Through this discussion students would organize their thoughts and gain new insights into the life of Christ which they may have previously overlooked. A few may actually learn new facts about Christ's life. But the primary purpose of a discussion is rarely to teach new factual information. Unless students have a base of knowledge from which to talk, their comments often have little significance.

Third, students can solve problems through discussion. Case studies, true or true-to-life situations which force students to analyze problems and discuss solutions, are examples of this function of discussion. Case studies are considered in greater detail later in this chapter.

Fourth, discussion stimulates creativity and aids students in applying what they have learned to everyday situations. For example, a teacher could give each student a foot-long piece of thin florist's wire and ask him to pretend this wire is a time line of his life the previous week. Every time the student remembers failing God he should put a bend in the wire.

After a few minutes, most of the students' wires would be twisted.

The class could then break into pair groups and discuss some of the problems Christians have that keep them from living in perfect fellowship with God. The Bible study might center on God's solution to this dilemma.

Fifth, when students verbalize what they believe and are forced to explain or defend what they say, their convictions are strengthened and their ability to share what they believe with others is increased.

MAKE DISCUSSION SUCCEED

The question or comment a teacher uses to start a discussion is very important because it sets the direction for what lies ahead. Discussion starters that begin with the words "Why?" "Explain," "What do you think?" are usually good because these words indicate that there is something to discuss.

Consider this discussion starter: "Retell the story of the feeding of the 5000 from the small boy's perspective." The student response might provide the class with a creative review, but the question probably will not start a discussion. However, on the same story, the teacher might ask, "When Jesus fed the 5000, He proved that He could feed a lot of people on a very low budget. But what does this story mean to us Christians who seldom see obvious miracles like this happen today?" Here the students must do more than repeat facts they have learned. There is something to discuss. Not only must they mentally review the story, but they are forced to analyze what it means. Again, students may interact as they answer, "Name Christ's 12 disciples and tell one important fact about each of them." But their comments only indicate that they have been listening to what you said. The question, "How were Jesus' 12 disciples a lot like we are today?" asks students not only to review what they have been taught but also to analyze how what they have learned applies to their contemporary situation.

The following discussion starters can be used in many different lesson situations to help students apply what they have studied:

1. If Christ were here today, what illustration or parable from contemporary life do you think He might use to help those around Him understand today's lesson? Explain your answer.

2. Let's discuss different ways we could put the lessons we have learned in today's Bible study to work in our lives.

3. How would you explain this passage to a non-Christian? To an elementary child?

Occasionally something will be said in a discussion to alert you to a need a student has that will not be met by the lesson you have planned. Because students always take precedence over lesson plans, you should switch the emphasis of your lesson to meet that need. For example, if during a discussion on living the Christian life a girl says, "I don't feel I can participate. I don't know Christ, and I'm not sure I want to. I just don't understand what's involved," the teacher should immediately respond to that girl's need by redirecting the discussion so Christian students will share what it means to accept Christ as Savior and Lord.

Sometimes even the whole direction of the lesson will need to be changed to meet the needs of the students. Consider what might happen if senior high teens enter their class talking about the accidental death of a boy who attended their high school. For the first time many of them may be asking mature and difficult questions about death. The teacher should realize that this is where his students' needs are. They are motivated to learn in this area. No matter how good the lesson he planned might be, he will fail as a teacher if he doesn't deal with the real problems his students are having. Discussion will probably play an important part in his unplanned lesson, but it should not take up the complete class hour. After students have shared their feelings, questions, and understanding about the Christian view of death, they will probably discover they still have doubts and unanswered questions. At this point the teacher should direct them to Biblical passages on the subject. Since he will not have prepared on this topic, he may not be familiar with all the relevant Scriptures. This gives him the perfect opportunity to teach his students how to use their Bible concordances. Discussion, Bible study, research, and possibly life response: they can all happen in an hour if a teacher remains sensitive to his students' needs.

No two people in a discussion are exactly alike. Each has biological and psychological needs, drives, patterns for living, past experiences, and creative abilities. Each should be encouraged to contribute in his unique way.

Some students will hesitate to speak in class because they are shy or feel their contributions are less valuable than those of their classmates. Draw them into the discussion by directing a question to them. Consider having them elaborate on something someone else has said, or ask them to share their opinions about a specific subject. "Marian," a teacher might say, "how do you feel about our local theater showing previews of restricted films before a feature that is designed for general audiences?"

Nearly every class has at least one member whose contributions do not seem as valuable as those of the rest of the class. Students should learn from your example how important it is to show respect for each person's comments. Sometimes a nod or a smile is all that is necessary to let the speaker and the rest of the class know you appreciate the contribution. Or, it may be possible to salvage something worthwhile from what the person has said and ask another student to comment or elaborate on that point.

No one should be allowed to monopolize the conversation. If it becomes obvious that this is happening, the teacher should politely cut that student's remarks and direct the conversation to another person: "Thank you, Mr. Johns, for your contribution. Mrs. Smythe, how do you feel about this point?"

Even if all students are participating, a discussion cannot be totally successful unless you maintain an atmosphere of freedom and inquiry. Each person must know that he is not required to make a "Sunday school response." Rather he should be able to share his true feelings and opinions during the discussion, even if they differ from traditional positions.

In a free discussion, you must assume the role of guide and participant rather than the role of an instructor or dictator. You steer, rather than shove, to keep the discussion relevant to the morning topic.

The success of a discussion depends on the people involved and the topic they are discussing, not on external variables such as the room arrangement. Even so the leader should try to make the classroom as conducive as possible to discussion.

Circles or semi-circles make the best seating arrangements because they eliminate the seat of authority. Students react directly with each other. No longer is the teacher the central figure in the room through whom all comments and questions must pass.

Also, in these arrangements, each person is able to see his classmates' expressions and reactions. This adds an additional dimension to the discussion.

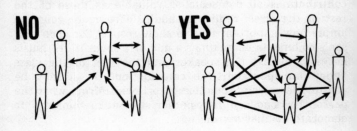

There is no room situation that cannot be adapted to discussion by a creative teacher. For example, a teacher in a classroom where desks and chairs have been nailed to the floor might ask some teens to turn sideways and others backwards in their chairs so they would all be facing each other. The teacher would then join the group, putting herself on the same level as her students so they could react and learn as equals who have things to contribute to each other.

Following every class period in which you use discussion, ask yourself these questions to help determine the success of the teaching method.

1. In what ways did this discussion contribute to my students' understanding of today's lesson? (Consider each student individually.)

2. In what specific ways did the students teach themselves during the discussion?

3. Was each person involved? If not, what can I do next time to correct this problem?

4. What follow-up, if any, should be made on the discussion? (For example, if students showed a lack of knowldege or misunderstanding in some area of Scripture, you may want to cover this subject soon during the class hour. Or, if students discussed decisions they were making or projects they felt the class should be involved in, follow-up outside the class hour may be necessary.)

METHODS OF DISCUSSION

TOTAL CLASS DISCUSSION

In some small classes, all students are able to participate in one effective discussion. But in most groups, total class discussion by itself is unsatisfactory because there is usually time for only a few to contribute. Also, many people who feel comfortable sharing with three or four others are inhibited by a larger group.

However, other types of discussion, such as buzz groups and brainstorming groups, conclude by having students return to total class discussion to report on what they have discussed. This gives the class a summary of everyone's input without sacrificing individual participation.

Buzz Groups

Small groups of from three to ten people are assigned any topic for discussion. They quickly select a chairman and a secretary. The chairman is responsible for keeping the discussion on the track, and the secretary records the group's ideas and reports the relevant ones when the buzz groups combine for total class discussion.

Brainstorming

Students, usually in small groups, are presented with a problem and asked to come up with as many different solutions as possible. The emphasis here is on quantity, not quality, based on the theory that quantity breeds quality. It's easier to modify a creative idea than it is to beef up an uncreative one. Participants should withhold judgment until all suggestions have been offered, or until about two-thirds of the time allotted to the brainstorming session has been spent. The group should then pick the best contribution from those suggested (or perhaps combine several different ideas) and refine it.

Each brainstorming group will present its solution in a total class discussion. If class action is indicated, the students may want to decide which idea they would like to further refine and act upon.

Consider using brainstorming problems like these:

1. Assume that we as Christians want to make an impact on our government. We have only the resources available to us that actually exist in this class. How can we best make this impact?

2. We feel strongly that as Christians we are responsible for the poor and are required to make some active response to better their condition. What can we do?

3. We would like to build better communications with (parents, children, neighbors, other churches). How can we go about doing this?

FORUM DISCUSSION

Forum discussion is especially valuable when:

1. The subject is difficult and the students would not be able to participate in a meaningful discussion without quite a bit of background.

2. People with special training or experience have insights which would not ordinarily be available to the students. Depending on the topic, it may not always be necessary for those participating in a forum discussion to be Christians.

Each forum member should prepare a three-to-five-minute speech, and be given uninterrupted time in which to present it. Then students should be encouraged to interact with the speakers, either directly or through a forum moderator—usually the teacher.

Adapt the following forum outlines to your class by substituting suggested participants with people available in your church and community.

Forum on drugs:
1. *Person who has tried and rejected the use of drugs*
2. *Doctor or police having experience with teens on drugs*
3. *Parent of a teen who is/was on drugs*

Forum on sex from a Christian perspective:
1. *Pastor or youth leader*
2. *Christian doctor*
3. *Christian parents (both a man and a woman), preferably with teenaged children*

Forum on race:
1. *Leader of a minority group in your community*
2. *Class members, especially if they are members of a minority group*
3. *Leader of a majority group in your neighborhood, perhaps the pastor.*

You will probably want to make your forum topics more specific than the ones provided here. Slant them so the speakers deal with problems that will help students better understand how the week's lesson applies to them.

For example, if the Scripture study dealt with the apostle Peter's difficulty accepting Gentile Christians, you might plan a forum on race and limit the general ideas just given. First you would set an aim stating what you want students to learn from the forum, and then you would assign specific topics to the speakers that would direct students toward the aim.

Forum on Race. Aim: to help us learn to be more Christian in our relationships with each other.

1. *Minority leader (Topic—areas in which I feel the need for change and suggestions on how to begin those changes.)*

2. *Class member (Topic—why I am proud of my color/ ethnic background; things the majority could learn from my people.)*

3. *Majority leader (Topic—areas in which I feel the need for change and suggestions on how to begin those changes.)*

Sometimes it is impossible for a person who could make an important contribution to your forum to be present. Suppose you wanted the head of the juvenile narcotics division of the city police force to participate in a forum for junior high and senior high students, but the officer had duty on Sunday morning. During the week before the forum, you or a student could interview the officer and record what he says. This is not an ideal situation, of course, because he won't be present for the response discussion. But the students will have the benefit of his insights, along with the other "live" members of the forum.

PANEL DISCUSSION

Panel discussions are held in much the same way as forum discussions, but they are less formal. Members from the audience may interrupt the speakers at any time after they have been recognized by the moderator.

And members of the panel may interact with each other.

Occasionally a lesson subject lends itself to debate. There are many ways to structure a debate, but during the Sunday school hour the following pattern is among the most effective. At least a week before the debate, those participating should be given the debate topic, stated in the form of a resolve. For example:

Resolved: Our church should take an active stand in our community and state on the race issue.

Resolved: Our class should begin a youth ministry centered outside the church (coffeehouse, bookstore, open house) to reach teens who would never participate in the organized church program.

As students prepare before class for their parts in a debate they should remember that it is the affirmative side's responsibility to prove that the resolve is correct. The negative has to prove that it isn't. Of course, the negative may also want to present an alternative proposal.

For example, in the youth ministry resolve, the negative may counter the affirmative's position with an objection like this: *our class members who would work in this ministry are not strong enough in their faith to work with street teens. They might end up being influenced by this group rather than influencing them for Christ.* Or, the negative may want to first discredit the resolve and then offer their own suggestion: *We believe we can initiate an extensive church sports program that would attract young people to our church.*

Constructive speeches (prepared speeches in which each debater states his part of the group's argument) should be from three to five minutes long. Rebuttal speeches (extemporaneous speeches in which debaters refute the other side's arguments) are usually only two or three minutes long.

Debaters should give their speeches in the following order:

1. First affirmative speech
2. First negative speech
3. Second affirmative speech
4. Second negative speech

(*Brief break while each side discusses and plans its rebuttal.*)

5. First negative rebuttal
6. First affirmative rebuttal
7. Second negative rebuttal
8. Second affirmative rebuttal

Since the burden of proof lies with the affirmative team, they have the advantage of presenting the first and last speeches. Debate winners are determined by the ability debaters show in presenting their positions. Simply stated, to win, the affirmative team must prove that the resolve is correct. To win, the negative team must prove that it isn't.

In a classroom debate it is often good to open the floor for comments and questions following the last rebuttal. The moderator should help direct these student remarks.

Mixed-Group Discussion

Often the Sunday school hour is so age-segregated that teens don't get to interact with their parents and other adults. The teens miss friendships that might build between them and the adults, and they are not exposed to the wealth of experience adults have. Adults miss the fresh ideas and approaches and the enthusiasm teens often have so much of.

Consider planning a mixed-group discussion when the aims of both groups' lessons are similar. For example, you might use the following mixed-group discussion idea or structure one like it for your adult and teen classes.

Parent-Teen Wisdom Exchange

(Adults who are not parents of teenagers should participate in the discussion in the way they think they would if they actually were parents of teens. Perhaps they might "adopt" for that Sunday teens whose parents do not attend the adult class.)

The dual aim for this program is to engage adults and teens in meaningful discussion of contemporary problems, and to develop greater understanding and appreciation for each other and for the wisdom recorded in the Book of Proverbs.

Participants should be challenged before the session to be honest with their comments and to come prepared to participate.

For the first part of the meeting, students should remain in their individual class groups. Give each group the same list of references on parent-child relationships and ask students to review them. The list may include: Proverbs 10: 13; 3: 12; 13: 22-24; 19: 18; 22: 6; 29: 15-17; Ephesians 6: 4; Proverbs 20: 7; 15: 5; 28: 7; 19: 26; 22: 15; 30: 11-17.

While they are still in their separate class groups, both groups should discuss how they would complete statements like these:

• The lesson stressed in these references that is most helpful to me right now is . . . because . . . .

• (Adult class) If I could teach a teen one lesson from these verses, (teen class) If I could teach a parent one lesson from these verses, I would teach . . . in the following way . . . .

Following the segregated discussions, the groups get together for summarizing how they answered the questions. Then the mixed-group discussion is ready to begin.

The discussion leader must point his questions toward both teens and adults. Otherwise, the session is likely to degenerate into a lecture aimed at the teens rather than a sharing time.

He may want to use questions like these to start discussion:

• Parents, in what areas do your teens still need instruction? How could this be given in a way the teens will accept?

63

• Teens, in what problem areas of your lives do you feel parents and Christian adults can be most helpful to you? Why and how?

• Teens, what types of correction do you feel are most helpful to you? Why?

• Parents, does your responsibility to correct ever end? Support your answer.

• Teens, what is the ideal relationship between parents and teens? What things often keep that ideal from becoming a reality?

Teens and adults may want to interact with each other's answers. Allow this discussion to continue for about ten minutes. Then reverse roles. Ask teens to pretend they are adults, and adults to play the role of teens. (Groups may need a few minutes at this time to review the Proverbs verses.)

The discussion leader should ask the same questions he did earlier, but this time the parents and adults will answer as teens, and the teens will be the parents.

If there are discrepancies between the original answers and the answers given by the roleplaying adults or teens, have the group stop and discuss the issue more fully.

The session should be concluded with a review of the evening given by both adults and teens. This summary could state what content has been learned or reviewed, and, in the opinion of those speaking, what the parent-teen exchange has accomplished.

INTERVIEW

The interview can be used by a teacher in several effective ways.

The interview as homework. Ask students to interview someone during the week and present what they learned in the form of short reports the following Sunday. In the simplest homework interview, the students ask the person they are interviewing a single question that has been supplied by the teacher. Then they write or verbally report in just a few sentences the responses they received.

A lot of the success of this mini-interview depends on the type of question the teacher assigns. It should be designed to force the people being interviewed to give a paragraph answer rather than a single word or phrase answer. Adapt the following ideas to fit your lesson aims.

• Talk with one person in our church neighborhood who does not attend church and ask him what his opinion of our church is and on what he bases that opinion.

• Interview someone who works on a volunteer basis in our church. Ask him what his job is and how we could make that job easier.

• Interview someone whose Christian life you admire. Ask him to share what led up to his accepting Christ as Lord of his life.

Older teens and adults are capable of doing more complete, in-depth interviews, but usually, because class time is limited, the single-question interview is the more effective teaching tool.

The interview in class. Occasionally it is profitable to schedule an in-class interview, perhaps with a visiting missionary or with someone who has unique insights to share with the group. An interview can often be more valuable to the class than a lecture given by that person, because, first of all, an interview demands student participation. And second, when students ask the questions, they are alerting the visitor to areas in which they have both interests and needs.

One person can take charge of the entire interview, structuring and asking questions. But whenever possible the entire class should take part. Each student should write one question he would like the guest to answer. Suggest he ask questions that require the speaker to talk in depth about his subject, and, whenever possible, deal with specifics rather than generalities.

A student could ask a Christian Peace Corps volunteer,

"How did you share the Christian life-style with people in your host country?" Or the class might benefit from knowing a foreign student's answer to, "What special problems do Christians in your country have?"

Members of large Sunday school classes could consider interviewing each other. They would set aside five minutes each class period in which to ask questions to a different classmate each week, in an effort to get to know one another better.

The in-group interview. Divide the class into groups of three, called triads. Supply all groups with the same question or discussion topic. A in the group interviews B and C listens. Then B interviews C while A listens. Finally C interviews A while B listens. Each interview should take from one to three minutes. When the triads return to the total class situation, each person reports on what he heard, not what he said.

Questions like these can be used in triad discussion:

• *Which story in the Bible means the most to you today? Explain why.*

• *What problem do you think Christians your age struggle with most, and what solution can you suggest?*

• *What can our church do to make singles feel more welcome?*

DISCUSSION BUILT AROUND A PICTURE/CARTOON/SONG

Some pictures look as if they could be the beginning of a story. All the teacher would have to ask is, "What happens next?" to lead his class into a creative discussion. A teacher might use a picture like the one at the top of the next page in a lesson on living the Christian life. After showing the class the picture, he could divide them into buzz groups and ask them to decide what happens next if only one teen in the picture is a Christian. There is no right or wrong conclusion to the picture story. Some groups may decide that the boy is a Christian, and when he sees his classmate cheating, he has a perfect opportunity to tell her about the difference

Christ could make in her life. Other groups may feel the girl is a Christian. When a boy she has been witnessing to sees her cheating he is no longer interested in hearing about her God.

Begin a collection of magazine pictures, photographs, and posters that can be used to focus the students' attention on a lesson and get them involved in discussion.

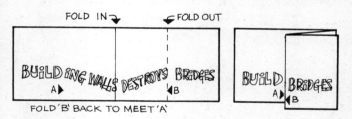

This poster can lead students to ask what walls they are building in their lives and how they can replace these walls with bridges.

Consider what might happen in an adult class discussion if the teacher displayed a picture she had clipped from a magazine of an unkempt teen, dressed in unconventional clothing, smoking a cigarette, and then asked her class, "Would he be welcome here?"

Cartoons can also be excellent discussion starters. The cartoon would be an effective way to get students interested in talking about what true spirituality is and how it should be evidenced in their lives.

Or, ask students to brainstorm ideas for an original cartoon caption. Prepare for this discussion by removing the caption from a cartoon that deals with the same subject you will be teaching. Sunday school publications and Christian magazines are good sources for cartoons with Christian themes. Preferably the cartoon you choose should not be familiar to your students.

Show the uncaptioned cartoon to the class. Then divide them into buzz groups. Ask each group to come up with a caption they think is funny and will teach others something about the truths the class has studied.

For example, following a lesson on stewardship, a junior high teacher might ask her students to write a caption for this cartoon.

As the students share their captions, ask questions like these:

- *Why do you think people sometimes learn more from cartoon messages than they do from sermons?*
- *What do you think a Christian would learn from reading this cartoon?*
- *Which of the groups' cartoons do you think is the best? Why?*

Music, like cartoons and posters, can also be used as a discussion starter. Occasionally a popular song will speak directly to the issues of a lesson.

Consider what might happen if in preparation for a lesson on maintaining Christian standards in the non-Christian world, a teacher asked his students to write and bring to class the words to their favorite popular songs. After the Bible study, he could divide the class up into buzz groups and give the following assignment: "Answer each of the four questions I will put on the chalkboard about the songs you have chosen."

1. What is each song saying about life?

2. As a Christian, can I accept this life view? Why or why not?

3. What questions, if any, are asked or implied in this song? What answers do I, as a Christian, have?

4. What rating, with ten as the best rating, would I give this song as to its value to me as a Christian? Explain your rating.

When the groups returned to total class discussion to talk about what they had learned, one teen could summarize his group's answer to question three: "All our songs were sad, so we figured the world must be looking for happiness and can't find it. We've found it in Christ, so I guess it's our duty to share."

Students' answers to question four would be very important. For example, a girl might share: "Sex was really an open thing in our songs, and when we read the words, we realized they glorified the wrong use of sex. We gave the songs a very low rating and thought it would be great to write a popular song of our own about the beauty there is in following God's rule."

Consider adapting the above idea to your class or develop one of these ideas.

• Play two or three Christian songs to illustrate different styles of music. Ask students to discuss the benefits and uses of each type.

• Develop a discussion around a new song you are teaching your class. For example, if the song were "They'll Know We Are Christians by Our Love," you might begin discussion of the first verse by asking, "In what ways is this verse a sermon? What community and national situations might arise that would cause a preacher to give a sermon like this one?"

DISCUSSIONS BUILT AROUND CASE STUDIES

In a case study, students analyze a true-to-life problem situation and usually suggest solutions to the problem. Through participating in synthetic situations, students gain skill in making decisions, appreciating the ways other people evaluate problems and find solutions, and picking the best of these solutions.

The abbreviated or embryo case study lends itself to class situations because it is easy to prepare and use. The teacher need only write the essential information for each case study on a card. Usually this will be no more than a few sentences. Ideas for abbreviated studies can come from items in the newspaper, advice columns, and real experiences.

Divide the class into small groups and supply each group with a copy of a case study. Then ask the students to follow these steps:

1. Read the case study and make sure each member of the group understands all the facts involved. (If at any time during the embryo study the group realizes it needs additional facts not provided on the card, they may agree to add them.)

2. Identify and agree on the problem. Often there will

be a surface problem which is just an indication of a much deeper one the group must find and discuss.

3. Suggest a number of solutions, perhaps in brainstorming fashion.

4. When all possibilities have been exhausted, determine the best solution(s) and share this solution with the total class.

In some case studies, students may want to put the solutions they have found into practice. (See "Case Study on Christian Service.") When this happens, encourage them to do so.

Introduce your class to discussion built around case studies by using one of the following examples, or use these examples as patterns for writing your own.

Case study on Christian Responsibility

Margaret wears shapeless and unfashionable dresses because she believes it is unchristian to draw any attention to her body. Joan realizes that Margaret is actually harming her testimony as well as the testimonies of the other Christian women in her neighborhood. Because of Margaret's example, they associate being a Christian with being slightly out of date. Joan feels it is her Christian responsibility to tell Margaret that she may actually be keeping people from coming to Christ. But when she explains to Margaret the difference between being tastefully attractive and being dowdy, Margaret gets angry and stalks away.

What are the problems here? What solutions can you suggest?

Case study on Christian growth

Jonathan recently accepted Christ, but his father, a member of an Eastern cult, refuses to allow him to attend church or associate with other Christians. Jonathan admits he has been having doubts about his salvation and is tempted to stop following Christ just to keep peace in the family.

What are the problems here? (Consider Jonathan's responsibility to be obedient to his father.) What solutions can you suggest?

Case study on Christian Service

Several teens are griping because they don't feel their wishes are considered when the adults make decisions concerning the church. Then one teen mentions that the young people haven't exactly been knocking themselves out contributing their time and money to the church. "Maybe this is why no one pays much attention to what we say," he notes. The group agrees and decides to plan ways they can get involved serving God through the church.

What ideas might the teens suggest? Point out the problems and the advantages of each suggestion.

5

GAMES

Lead your class in a roleplay simulation...

Because they are fun, games motivate students. In the game atmosphere even slow learners become involved and learn much more than they do in other, more traditional situations.

Very broadly, there are two types of games. First, there are those which are competitive. Participants follow the rules and work toward a pre-specified goal. Second, there are those which are known by the interchangeable terms: socio-drama, simulation, and gaming. These games try to reproduce some aspect of reality—poverty situations, power struggles in government, ecological problems, etc.—so the people participating will be better able to understand that one life area, and perhaps through understanding they will make better, wiser decisions within that area.

DEVELOP AN ORIGINAL COMPETITIVE GAME

Junior high and senior high students will enjoy developing and playing their own competitive Bible games. (Often adults do not. Many feel threatened by the value placed on content knowledge.)

Read the directions to the game, Bible Basketball, to your class after you have completed a unit of study. Have each student help complete the game by writing three content questions about the Bible lessons the class has just studied. Then play the game as a review.

Or the class could use the ideas in Bible Basketball as an idea-starter and develop its original sports review game. For instance, ask students what rules might be needed to make a game of Bible Hockey, Bible Soccer, or Bible Checkers. The students' imaginations will be the only limitations on these original game possibilities.

Bible Basketball

Each student should write three or more review questions. The teacher shuffles these and picks questions at random.

The class divides into two teams. The teacher asks a tip-off question, and the first team to answer correctly gets the first chance to sink a basket.

The teacher then reads the first game question to the team that answered the tip-off. If the team players answer without being blocked by the other team, they score two points. If they give no answer, they neither score nor lose points.

After the tip-off question the teams alternate opportunities to make baskets.

Blocking: After each answer, the teacher gives the opposing team an opportunity to say whether the answer just given is incorrect. If students say that it was incorrect, they have blocked the answer. If their accusation is correct, the other team does not score and the blocking team gets one point and an opportunity to correctly answer the question. If they give the right answer, they earn another point. If they give an incorrect answer, they neither gain nor lose a point. However, if they have incorrectly blocked and the answer given by the other team was correct, the blocking team fouls and loses two points.

If the original answer was incorrect but the opposing team does not block it, the teacher gives the correct answer and the team giving the incorrect answer is allowed to keep the two points it scored.

(Additional rule for advanced players: each team member must take his turn answering a question. No member may answer a second time until each player has answered once.)

74

A winning team is declared at the end of a designated time or when one team obtains a certain number of points.

SIMULATION GAMES— DESIGNED FOR EXPLORATION

Basically, all games which fit into this category try to simulate reality, make it simpler than what it is, reduce its size so players will better understand the aspect of reality covered in the game.

A student, through these games, experiments with life. For example, he might play a politician who must please both his conscience and his constituency, or a scientist who must deal with pollution problems. Simulations, like roleplay, are one step removed from reality. This minimizes the sense of risk. A student feels free to participate and learn through involvement because he realizes the situation isn't real life.

Simulations can lead a student to think deeply about issues that were previously only words. It's easy for him to yell, "I made it by myself. Why can't they?" until he has participated in an inner-city poverty simulation and realized some of the pressures and frustrations of being manipulated by those with money and influence. When a student learns to examine issues rather than yell slogans, he is beginning to develop skills in decision making, communicating, and understanding people.

Simulation is a potential attitude changer. If after playing a game a student better understands how government works, he may want to participate in its functions. Or when a student takes part in a Christian simulation, such as the game of *Guidance* included in this chapter, he may gain the confidence he needs to begin to help others. Simulation leads to personal growth when a student begins to practice positive things he learned in the game; or to work to eliminate the negative things such as prejudice and misused power he saw demonstrated.

There are, however, several problems associated with using simulation in a Sunday school situation.

Most simulations require at least an hour's playing time with additional time following the game for discussion.

Also most games require a lot of space and a large number of people.

Many simulation games are priced beyond the church budget.

And, although many of the secular simulation games have a lot to teach Christians, students and teacher will have to structure their own discussion to include the Christian implications of the game, since guidelines for this type of investigation are not given. (For descriptions of many simulations now available, see *The Guide to Simulation/Games for Education and Training,* compiled by David W. Zuckerman and Robert E. Horn and published by Information Resources, Inc., P.O. Box 417, Lexington, Massachusetts 02173.)

Quite often the teacher will find that the benefits students gain from a simulation experience far outweigh the problems that must be overcome.

A COMPLETE ROLEPLAY SIMULATION GAME—GUIDANCE

Introduce your students to simulation by teaching them to play *Guidance.* This game is developed around roleplay situations. In each, a person with a problem asks a Christian for help. The way in which the Christian helper deals with both the person and his problem is evaluated and rated by each student in class.

Incorporate this game into your teaching plans when lessons deal with how Christians can put Biblical principles to work in today's life situations.

Guidance is designed to help your students:

• Analyze the opportunities they have to help others and react correctly to these opportunities.

• Develop sensitivity to others.

• Discover more about how God works through Christians to accomplish His purposes.
 • Develop their knowledge of the Bible so they can use it effectively in everyday situations.

Playing Data

Age Level: Junior high through adult. (Before the game is played, the teacher should read all Situation Cards and delete any that do not apply to the age level he is teaching.)

Number of Players: Two roleplayers and any number of evaluators.

Playing Time: Minimum, 15 minutes; no maximum.

Preparation

Cut out the Situation and Attitude Cards printed on pages 83 through 109.

Reproduce a large number of Guidance Score Cards from the sample printed on page 79. Each evaluator will need one Guidance Score Card for every roleplaying situation he witnesses.

Be thoroughly familiar with how the game is played before your students play it. If necessary, review the principles of effective roleplay with your students. (See chapter 1.)

Playing Directions

Although the whole class participates in playing *Guidance,* the burden of each roleplay situation falls on two students. One will play the Christian helper and the other the problem student. The problem student chooses a SITUATION card and reads it to the helper and the group. Then the problem student takes an ATTITUDE card. Without revealing the information on this card until the roleplay is over, he assumes the attitude suggested on the card.

Each roleplay situation asks or implies a question. The session should begin with the Christian helper asking the problem student two or three questions to gain a greater understanding of the problem and to get an idea of the attitude of the problem student. After he has this basic information, he is ready to deal with the problem situation.

Although the problem student has the stronger acting part, it is the ability of the Christian helper to aid the problem student in working out a Christian solution that is being judged by the class.

Each class member should be given an EVALUATION card on which he will rate the helper from one to five points in four categories. Five are the most points a helper can earn in any category with the exception of two bonus points for using a relevant Scripture verse in the roleplay.

Guidance Score Cards
Points are scored in the following areas:
Effective use of Bible—5 points or less
  (bonus 2 points for effective use of reference)
Personality understanding—5 points or less
Biblical carry-over—5 points or less
Practical suggestions—5 points or less
A perfect score is 20.

Before the game begins, explain the significance of each scoring category.

Effective use of Bible—In *Guidance,* the helper must use Biblical principles correctly. Often the helper will not be able to quote the verse verbatim, but the game assumes that if the helper knows what the Bible says on the subject, he would in a real-life situation be able to use a concordance to find the specific verse. However, if a helper is able to use any relevant verse, explain the message it contains, and give the reference, he scores an extra two bonus points.

At least one Biblical reference is given on each Situation card; however, these verses do not contain the total answers to the problems. They may be used as a starting basis if any student would like to study a situation more completely. The principles found in the Bible, when

Effective use of Bible:
5 points or less
(Bonus: 2 points for
effective use of
reference)

Personality understanding:
5 points or less

Biblical carry-over:
5 points or less

Practical suggestions:
5 points or less

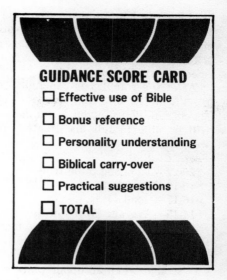

GUIDANCE SCORE CARD

☐ Effective use of Bible

☐ Bonus reference

☐ Personality understanding

☐ Biblical carry-over

☐ Practical suggestions

☐ TOTAL

applied to any life situation, offer a sound base from which Christian decisions can be made and problems solved.

Personality understanding—This category demands that the helper understand the attitude of the student. It keeps the helper from being more interested in the problem than in the person he is helping. It is an exercise in awareness.

Often the problem student will accept or reject advice on the basis of how the helper approaches his problem. The attitude of the problem student determines the helper's approach.

Biblical carry-over—This simply means putting the Bible into life today. It is the application part of the roleplay. The helper must show first what the Biblical principle is and then show how this principle fits the problem of the other student.

Practical suggestions—In this area the helper gives the

problem student some positive steps for action. For instance, if the problem is his devotional life, the helper might suggest the two of them have partner devotions for a few weeks to share what they have learned in some specific part of the Scripture.

After the roleplay is concluded—the average roleplay runs from three to four minutes—observers fill out their sheets. These are given to the helper, and from them he will be able to tell his greatest areas of strength and weakness.

Score Evaluation

20-22—Too good to be true.

18-19—Excellent.

16-17—Good.

14-15—Average. Work on lowest areas.

12-13—Fair. Practice a few more roleplays to bring up your score.

11 or below—Poor. Work hard to improve your score so that when an opportunity arises, you'll be able to give God your best.

For students to get the maximum benefit from playing *Guidance,* discussion must follow every situation. The value of the situation to the group and what happened in the roleplay should determine the amount of time spent on the discussion—usually from three to ten minutes.

Discussion should include questions like these:

• (To the Christian helper) What clues did you pick up from the problem student that told you how to deal with him? (To the total class) What additional clues did you see?

• In what ways did the helper show his understanding of the problem?

• What was the most effective thing the helper did in this situation? Why?

• What would you have done differently? Why?

• If you had been the problem student, how would you have reacted to the helper? Why? How do you think a person with this problem in real life might have reacted? Why?

- What principle(s) for helping others did you see demonstrated in this roleplay? (If you will be doing a number of *Guidance* situations, list these principles on a chalkboard.)
- What additional Scripture could you suggest? Explain your choice. (Consider writing these suggestions on the Situation card.)

When your students are familiar with this roleplay simulation, they may want to add additional Situation and Attitude cards to help them gain roleplay practice in other areas of their Christian lives.

For example, *Guidance* doesn't deal directly with witness situations and touches only briefly on interpersonal relationship situations. These would be excellent areas in which your students could expand their game. Suggest they write each original situation on one side of a 3 x 5 card and each attitude on one half of a 3 x 5 card. This will limit the size of the situations and keep the new game cards uniform.

Challenge your students to write situations which are complex enough to simulate real-life situations. No Situation card should be included in the game until at least one relevant Scripture reference has been included on it. This will force students to get into Biblical research and at least begin to find answers to their own roleplay problems.

GUIDANCE

A Roleplay Game

Cut apart the following Attitude cards for use in Guidance roleplay simulation.

Ready for change in life. Anxious to ask questions.	Tired of struggling. Hoping for solution.
Desperate for an answer. Anxious to listen.	Sarcastic. Determined to counter all helper's suggestions with biting remarks.
Discouraged. Doubting salvation because of problem. (Lead helper to this deeper problem.)	Worried. Anxious for someone to help you change this attitude.
Disinterested in finding solution. Merely talkative.	Argumentative. Unable to believe an answer is available.
Amazed to find someone who really cares.	Scared the helper will reject you as a person because of your problem.

Unhappy. Too tied up in self to see God's way out.

Physically, emotionally tired. Not concentrating.

Excited by the possibility of a solution.

Doubtful if suggestion will work. Willing to try.

Determined not to be influenced by Christian helper.

Hesitant. Unable to believe God guides life.

Upset with self for sharing. Resentful of helper.

Unhappy with self and life in general.

Embarrassed. Feeling foolish for not being able to solve own problems.

Afraid. Want God to rule life but scared to try.

Happy to find someone who cares. Anxious to listen.	Pessimistic about life. Certain any solution will fail.
Impressed with own Bible knowledge. Inattentive.	Worried that any solution will just lead to another failure.
Argumentative. Want to argue more than find solution.	Polite, but not overly interested in finding a solution.
Embarrassed by religious talk. Try to change subject.	Busy, hurried, anxious to hear simplest solution in shortest amount of time.
Fearful of exposing too much of self. Anxious to change subject.	Resentful of anyone who tries to help.

Anxious to find easy solution. Lazy, not willing to work at it.	Joking. Just kidding the helper about the problem. Whole thing is put-on.
Resentful. Fighting changes in your life you know God wants.	Angry. Blaming God for problem.
Embarrassed. Joking to hide importance of issue from helper.	Doubtful if any solution will work in this difficult situation.
Frightened. Afraid you will fail.	Optimistic. Looking for a workable solution to problem.

Cut apart the following Situation cards for use in Guidance roleplay simulation.

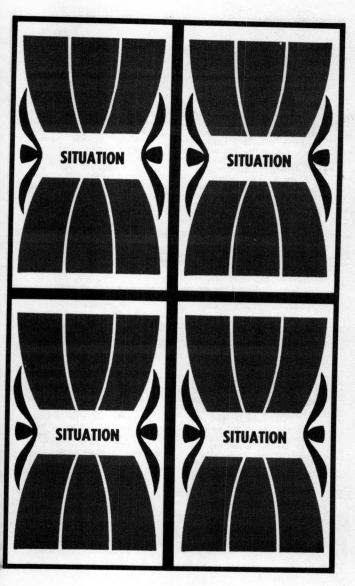

Before I became a Christian, I had the habit of shoplifting small items. Since I met Christ, I repaid the merchants from whom I stole. But I know a number of my non-Christian friends are still playing the shoplifting game. If I report them, I lose the opportunities I have been having to witness to them; and if I don't, I'm living as though I approve of what they're doing. How in the world does a Christian handle a problem in which any way he goes seems half wrong?
(Ephesians 4: 28; I John 5: 4)

I've always thought God was guiding me to be a medical missionary, but today I discovered that I'm flunking biology. No nursing school would take a chance on me now. What happened to what I thought was God's will? I feel like God failed me, and I wish you could prove to me that I'm wrong.
(James 1: 5; I Peter 4: 10)

I've never said I hate my parents but inside I know I do. God says we should honor them, and He even promises long life if we do. I've asked Him to help me see them as lovable people, but whenever we're together, we blow up at each other. So what am I supposed to do to change both our attitudes?
(John 13: 34)

I've always heard that God takes care of those who love Him. And I believed it until I discovered my father/husband/wife (choose one) has cancer. Short of a miracle, he/she is going to die. And I need him/her. What good is being a Christian if I can't depend on God to pave my way? How is God any better to me than He is to people who consider His name nothing more than a swear word?
(I Peter 5: 8-10)

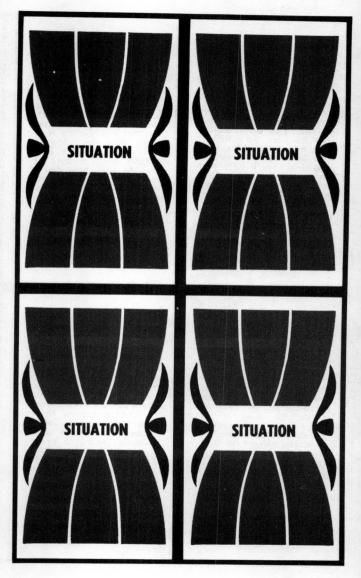

My kid brother is into drugs, and our folks don't know. I hate to be responsible for my brother's life, even though I know he is ruining it. He claims to be a Christian, but he sure isn't living like one. I love him, but if I tell the folks about the drugs, he'll hate me forever. How can God help me guide my brother? Is doing my duty more important than saving his love for me?
(II Thessalonians 3: 14, 15)

I can't think of a single prayer of mine that God has answered. In fact, He's been so silent that I'm not really sure He's there. Well, deep down I believe it, but He just doesn't seem a part of my life now. How can I make God speak up loud enough for me to hear and understand Him?
(Hebrews 11: 6)

20)

There is no way I can get to college. My folks can't send me; I'm not smart enough to get a merit scholarship or poor enough to get a help scholarship. Grades come hard for me, so I couldn't work and study at the same time and expect to graduate. This might limit what I can do for God, but I figure if He can't get me an education, it lowers my obligation to Him. If life is unfair to me, why should I cooperate with the God who allows it to be that way?
(Matthew 25: 14-30)

I can't believe that all the things my Christian friends say are wrong really are. Does God expect me to think exactly the way they think? Does He just speak to them and not to me? Sometimes I am sure God wouldn't mind If I did a certain thing and they are just as sure He would. How can I know what God thinks?
(I Peter 2: 21; I John 3: 20, 21)

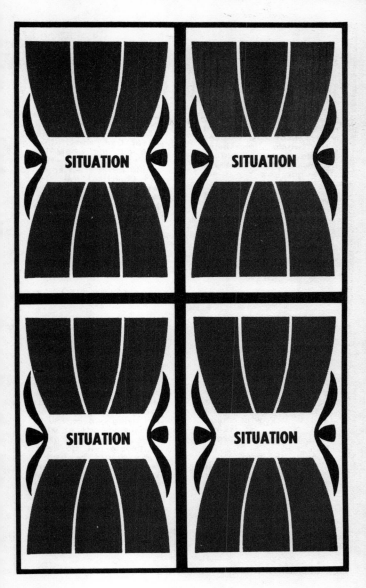

I promised the Lord I would have devotions every morning if it killed me, and to be honest, it just about has. I spend the whole time being bored. Sure, I want to know God's will for my life, but how can I get to know Him well enough to find out what it is without falling asleep in the process?
(Psalm 71: 23)

Cheating has become a way of life for me, and even though I know it's wrong, I don't see how I can stop without hurting my testimony. You see, people respect me because I always succeed. They listen when I talk about God, and if they find out my whole life has been a lie, they would never trust another Christian. My life would be a less effective witness if I were honest. I know this is wrong reasoning, but what can I do to keep my sin from damaging how non-Christians feel about God?
(Ephesians 4: 28; Romans 2: 21, 24)

One of the men in our group figured God was important in every area of his life except the sexual part. Now he's contracted venereal disease and is sick with shame and worry. He thinks God will never forgive him, and he's sure the people he loves won't. What can I do to help him and get him back to the place where God can use him again?
(II Chronicles 30: 9; Romans 6: 19)

The sections I read in the Bible never seem to have anything to do with the life I lead after devotions are finished. I feel as if I'm being hypocritical to have devotions at all— they just aren't as great as people tell me devotions should be. But I feel guilty if I miss them. What are real devotions anyway, and how can I have them?
(II Timothy 2: 15)

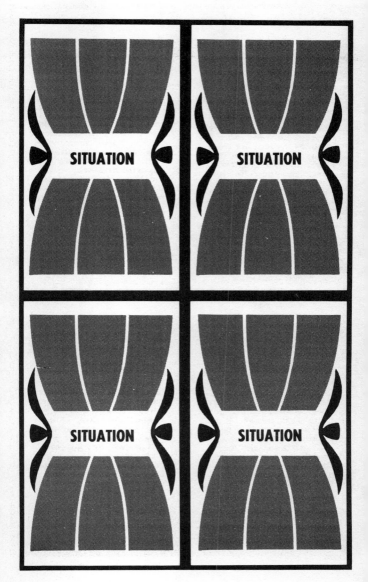

I've been a Christian for years, and it's a little hard to take God as seriously as the people who have recently met God. Their lives were pretty messed up, and Christ brought about a big change for them. God works in new Christians' lives, and my life just plods along in the same humdrum way it always has. How can I get more enthusiastic about my Christian life?
(Psalm 51: 8, 12)

Inside my head, I'm a great conversationalist. But when I have to get the words out where someone else can hear them, I turn quiet and even mousy. I wish God would make me more like what I am on the inside so I could use the opportunities He gives me. Now, for instance, instead of witnessing, I turn clammy. What can I do to help God turn me into the type of person I want to be?
(Psalm 28: 7)

I'm seriously interested in going into politics. I know there are few people who can live a Christian testimony in the political world. Do you think that might be an indication that this occupation is outside the will of God? If so, why would God have given me the abilities and desires I have? How can I know God's will?
(Romans 12: 2; Psalm 18: 4-9)

I blow my stack over the least little thing. People make one wrong move, and I explode and make enemies for life. Unless I can control my temper, I am of little use to God. But it will mean a complete personality change, and how in the world can I do that?
(Proverbs 10: 14, 31, 32)

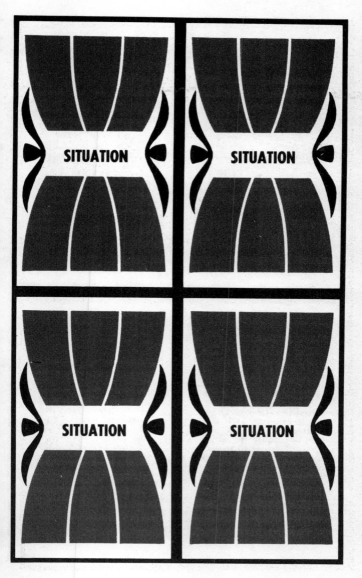

99

I avoid and even fear people who are different than I am in race, color, or even the part of town they come from. I know God doesn't like my attitude. But all my friends feel the same way, and I don't see how I can break a pattern I've lived in ever since I was a kid. I know being a Christian should help me, but exactly how does it?
(Luke 18: 9-14)

I have two non-Christian friends who have been living together. They've finally decided to get married and have asked me to be in the ceremony. If I accept I'm afraid the teens in my neighborhood who know I'm a Christian will think I'm condoning premarital sex. On the other hand, I have had several opportunities to share Christ with this couple. I wouldn't want to destroy our friendship by refusing to be part of their wedding. What should I do?
(Titus 2: 7, 8)

Since my parents aren't Christians, I feel God has given me the job of winning them for Him. But I've been living the Christian life for two years without seeing a single result. It's just as if God isn't helping at all, and I'm beginning to think He's unfair not to answer my prayer for their salvation. How long does God expect me to wait and how can I keep being a consistent witness?
(Colossians 4: 2)

For the last few years of school I've been dating the same person, and we are planning to be married after graduation. But my folks feel we haven't given God time to show us what His perfect will is. Don't you think that in three years God would have had time to show us if we are wrong? Isn't the fact that we love each other enough of an indication of God's will?
(Proverbs 15: 21, 22)

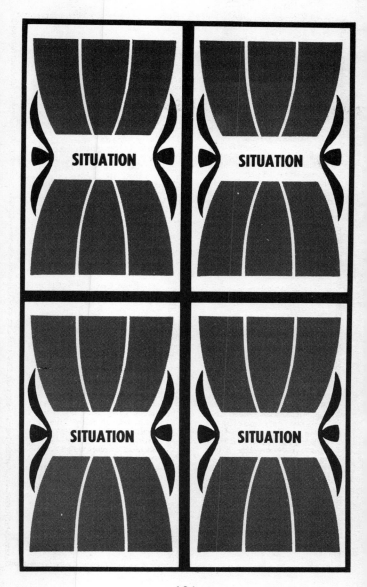

I have a bad heart and the least amount of exercise wears me out. I want to do what I can for God, but because of my handicap, I wonder how much He expects of me. When I think of the energy some people can devote to the Lord, I'm defeated before I begin. How much use can I be to God, who can use any healthy Christian He pleases to get the job done faster?
(Psalm 94: 17, 18; I Peter 4: 10)

Years ago we promised to love each other forever, and we were sure of our decision. But now we've divorced. This has really made me think about the permanence of love. How can I be sure that God will continue to love me throughout my life? Maybe His love will end like my partner's love did when things got rough?
(Jeremiah 31: 3)

I don't believe I should live for money, but I do think it's stupid not to try to be a financial success. Here's my problem. On the one hand, I feel God wouldn't want me to settle for less than I could make, and from this I would give Him His share. But on the other hand, I've always felt there was something spiritual about being poor. How can I keep from feeling guilty about being a success?
(Matthew 25: 14, 15, 19-21)

I've heard it said that I should love God more than anything else in life. When I'm honest, I know that I don't. I don't spend time with Him or think about Him like I would if He were really all-important to me. How can God expect us to care about Him as much as we do for people we can see and touch? Isn't He setting a standard no one can reach?
(I John 5: 1-3)

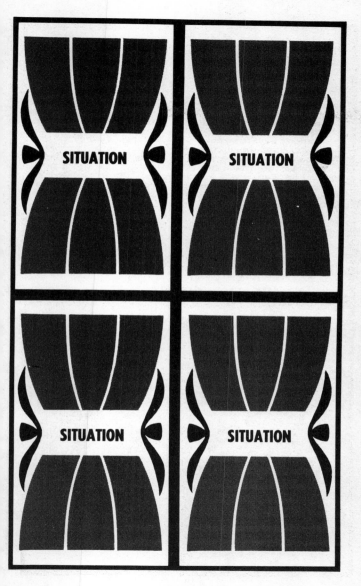

Last week I ruined my testimony so badly that people I didn't even know made snide remarks like, "If you're a Christian, I wouldn't want to be one." God's cause would have gone ahead a lot faster without me. How can I ever be of any use to God again? Will God ever forgive me for failing Him so completely?
(Psalm 25: 7, 11, 18; I John 2: 1, 2, 12)

It seems to me God has picked favorites just like everyone else in the world. Take money, for instance. I don't have enough to buy a complete lunch tomorrow, and yet I'm supposed to accept this with a smile. Well, how can God expect a hungry Christian to really love and follow Him?
(Philippians 4: 19; Acts 2: 44, 45)

If God gave us love, how can any expression of love be wrong? What harm is there in sleeping with someone I love, especially now that unwanted pregnancies are no longer the problem they used to be? Why can't I satisfy my needs and live a completely useful Christian life at the same time?
(Hebrews 13: 4)

Most Christians at my church are hypocrites, and I am less than excited about associating with them. I think it would be more of a worship experience for me to stay away from church and pray at home. Isn't it possible that once I got away from these people who are such pains God would be better able to speak to me? What value is there in my continuing to come to church?
(I John 4: 20; Romans 14: 10)

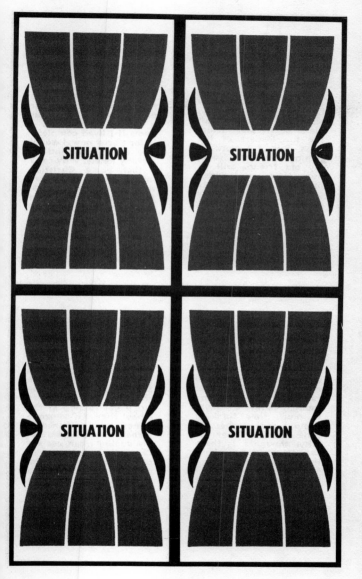

Most of my school friends aren't popular. I know God has given me the ability to fit in with all kinds of people, including the leaders of the class. But if I work at joining the "in" group, my old friends will be hurt. How can I widen my circle of friends without hurting or losing my old friends?
(Matthew 25: 40)

Right now it's very important for me to be a part of my group. I've read that this need for group identity lessens as a person gets older. I know if I lived completely for Christ now, I would lose my friends and be awfully lonely. Why can't I just be a Christian inside now and save the out-and-out dedication until I'm older and it will be easier to make a stand?
(Proverbs 1: 10)

I want God to rule my life, and I think I'm fair when I say He does rule my actions. But how can I let Him rule my thought life? I spend so much time thinking about sex that there is little time left over for other thoughts. Is there something sinful about the sex drive? Should I try to control what I think about, or doesn't it matter?
(Philippians 4: 8)

I'm the type of person who always plays second fiddle. If I get invited to a party, it's because someone else canceled out. I get to sing in the school chorus if someone comes down with a sore throat. I don't have a single quality I can use for Christ that someone else doesn't have more of. I'm discouraged. How does a second fiddle fit into God's plan?
(Luke 22: 27)

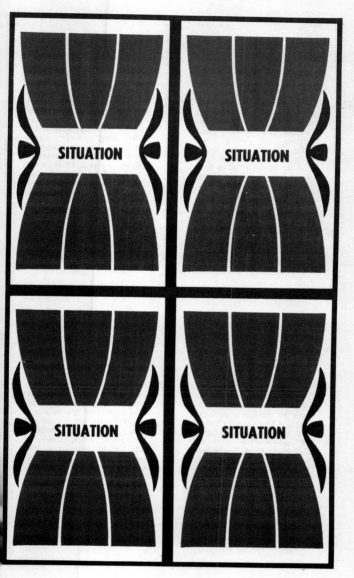

It seems to me that the most dynamic Christians I know are either good looking or very outgoing. I'm neither, but I really want to serve God. How do you suppose God would use a person like me?
(Romans 12: 4, 5)

I don't think I have a single friend who doesn't know I'm a Christian. But even though I talk a lot about God and what I believe, I've never led one person to Christ. My witnessing never turns out the way it does in most of the Christian stories I read. Is it possible that God doesn't want me to witness? If He does, why doesn't He make my efforts more successful?
(Galatians 2: 20; Acts 4: 20)

Before I can really let God rule my life, do I have to go back and correct all the wrong things I've ever done? What is my association with my past now that I'm a new person?
(Psalm 32: 5)

I dislike myself. In fact, there isn't one thing about me I admire. I hear people say God loves me and can lead me in a successful, useful life of service. But I can't believe He really cares. If He did, He would help me like myself better. I wish you could prove to me that I'm worth liking.
(Mark 3: 35)

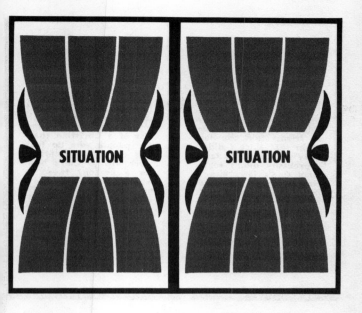

It's great to be in control of a speeding car. I know I often break speed limits, but I rarely do anything really dangerous. A friend told me last night that since I didn't obey my country's laws, I probably didn't really obey God's laws either. How can he relate speeding to Christianity? Isn't he being overly religious? (John 12: 26)

I have no desire whatsoever to go into full-time Christian work, and sometimes I get the feeling that this makes me less of a Christian than the people who do feel this calling. Is full-time work always God's best for a person? If so, I want it, but how can I get the desire to do it? If it isn't, how can I get rid of my guilt feelings? (Galatians 6: 4)

6

CREATIVE WRITING

Pencil plus paper equals results...

When a student picks up a pencil and puts his thoughts on paper, some very exciting things can happen to both him and those who share his creation.

• *Creative writing assignments can help a student stabilize in his own mind what he believes.*

Encourage a student to write in the first person—"I believe," "I feel." This helps him communicate more personally and honestly and forces him away from safe generalities—"We believe," "We feel."

• *A student who may have considered himself untalented in this area can often have a successful experience with simple creative writing assignments.*

The discovery of his ability to communicate through writing gives the student a sense of achievement which few other teaching methods can match.

• *His creative writing offers the student a permanent record of his thoughts, ideas, decisions.*

Of course, most writing which he does in class will not have lasting value to the student, but if he should create a poem, song, prayer that touches him, he will be able to keep that piece, and perhaps polish it and share it with others outside his class.

A group of teens, children of missionaries to Japan, were able to do just that. Each wrote a paragraph explaining why he was proud of his father.

Then all it took was a little polishing and a few transitional sentences to turn their paragraphs into an article they hoped would help other teens appreciate their Christian parents more. The following excerpts are from their article, "It Takes a Man," as it was published in a senior high Sunday school paper:

"My father is often a complete failure," grinned Mark DeShazer, a senior at a school for missionary children near Tokyo. "And I think that proves his courage, faith, and Christian manhood more than anything else.

"You see, it's no great thing to be dedicated to a job when the world says it's important and it applauds you verbally and financially. But sometimes he sees no results. The world sneers and says he's wasting his life and education on a fruitless task. His family goes without things other men can give their loved ones. When his only justification for being on the mission field is a command from God which the world discounts as foolishness, that's courage."

Eighth-grader Susie summed up the qualities of manhood necessary for success in God's foreign service when she described her father, Herb Murata. "My father is sort of a second fiddle. He does odds and ends which don't seem of real importance, but are, if everything in our ministry is to run smoothly. He honestly enjoys his work and does it well. I'm proud of him. I have a right to be, because in his attitude and understanding, in his love for God and the people God has given him to work with, my dad is the biggest man I know."

• *A student is able to learn from his classmates as each person shares his creative writing.*

For example, the new Christian may increase his knowledge about his Savior and have some of his ideas clarified and questions answered as he reads what his classmates have written.

Those students who have been Christians for a long

time get the benefit of the enthusiasm and fresh approach which is often a part of the new Christian's writing. A new Christian may not be familiar with the "Christian" cliches many students use to express spiritual things, and so often he writes in more personal and creative ways about what God means to him.

For example, a 15-year-old girl with little Christian background wrote how she felt about God in the following poem.

> I am the grass in the field, Lord.
> And You are the great, blue sky.
> Wind tries to blow me down,
> Rain hits me hard.
> But I am trying to grow higher and higher
> Into the blue Heaven, Lord.

• *A student may feel more secure writing and reading his thoughts to his classmates than he does taking part in a discussion and other extemporaneous activities.*

For example, many students are hesitant about talking aloud to God, yet they want to participate in group prayer. When they write their prayers, they have time to organize their thoughts. Gone is the worry about what words they will speak next. They are free to concentrate on what they are saying to God.

The following poem and prayer were candid, honest thoughts written and read to God by seventh graders following a lesson on spiritual battles.

POEM: *I'm in the Army.*
    The Lord is my Captain.
    We went to war with Satan.
    My Captain charged while I napped.
    The Lord came back all beaten and worn.
    He stopped in front of me and said,
     "You lost."

PRAYER: *Lord, I just lost my fight.*
     I found that I didn't really
      want to win.

Help me, Lord.
My battle is homework.
I hate it, and I'm so lazy.
I really don't want to work.
Help me, Lord, to be on the job.
Next time make me sit down.
Don't let me goof around.

• *Creative writing homework assignments can help a student prepare for his lesson during the week so he arrives in class ready to both participate and learn.*

These assignments can have outreach value in homes where not all members are interested in the church. Mrs. Jones may not want her daughter to share the plan of salvation with her, but she might read a poem her daughter wrote on the subject.

• *Through his creative writing a student shows his teacher where he is in his spiritual growth and often alerts the teacher to problems he is having.*

For example, one teacher asked her class to write an ending to the following statement: "The most important thing I learned during my study of the Ten Commandments is . . . ." A girl from a non-Christian background wrote, "I learned that your God is a very demanding God. I like His rules, but I could never live like that. I am not made like Him. I am sorry." From this comment, the teacher realized that she had not stressed God's love enough or made God's plan of salvation clear.

TRY SOME OF THESE CREATIVE WRITING IDEAS IN YOUR CLASS

Many of the following ideas can be completed in a few minutes of class time. Some of them may be more valuable as homework assignments which students complete during the week and bring to class to share with each other.

Choose the idea you will use with care. Before you decide on a method, ask yourself, "How does this writing activity fit into my lesson plan? How will it help my students better understand and apply the lesson?"

There are numerous ways to adapt a method for use in a lesson. For an example of how one writing idea can be expanded in many different ways, see page 116.

These class writing ideas are just that—ideas. Start with the idea given here, and be creative!

POETRY
ACROSTIC POEMS

In an acrostic, the words are arranged in a certain order so that specific letters in each line—usually the first or the last—form a pattern or spell a word or motto. A popular Old Testament poetic form, the acrostic was used by the psalmist in Psalms 9, 25, 34, 37, 111, 112, 119, and 145.

Students can build acrostics by using the alphabet.

Example 1
   A—Always
   B—Believe
   C—Christ

Example 2
   A—All my life I will praise You, Lord,
   B—Because You have shown Your love to me,
   C—Caring for me when I least deserve it.
Students can also build acrostics around key words in their lesson.

Example 3
   J—Jesus, You are always near;
   O—Oh, how great to know
   Y—You will never fail me.
The acrostic is an excellent method to use with adults (who are perhaps ill at ease with putting their ideas in writing) because it gives them a structure to follow. Suggest that if they can't think of a word, phrase, or sentence to follow a letter, they should go on to the next

line. Explain that a student will be asked to share only a line rather than his entire acrostic. This makes the project less threatening.

Examples of Different Ways to Use an Idea
—Built around the Acrostic

1. After the Bible study, divide the class into small Poem Power groups. Ask each group to develop an original acrostic built around the theme of the lesson: for example, PRAYER, LOVE, SALVATION, PRAISE. Then have each group read its poem to the rest of the class.

This same idea can be adapted for use with students who have reading/writing deficiencies. Write the acrostic word or phrase vertically on the chalkboard. Have students suggest phrases to follow each letter, and you write them on the board. The finished poem will be just as meaningful to the students as one they wrote completely by themselves.

2. Use an acrostic at the beginning of a lesson and at the end to provide a study in contrast. For example, if the lesson were on Christ's solution for sin, the class could begin by writing acrostics using and defining the words "SIN," or "EVIL." The period could end with the students expressing thanksgiving to God for His solution by writing acrostics from the words "SALVATION," or "GOOD."

Or the contrast could be obtained by using the same word. For example, at the beginning of an Easter lesson, students would write acrostics explaining what that holiday means to non-Christians:

E—*Each of us buys something new to wear.*
A—*All the children get candy-filled baskets.*

After studying the Christian's reason for celebrating Easter, students could write what it means to them:

E—*Every time I think of Christ's resurrection*
A—*And remember He was raised for me, I am thrilled!*

3. As homework in a junior high or senior high class,

ask students to write an acrostic around the Bible story they will be studying the following week. This is a unique way to introduce some students to the story and to get others who are already familiar with it to review. Then when the students get to class, they can quickly share their acrostics and be ready to study the lesson on a deeper-than-story level.

In the story of Samuel and Eli, the acrostic could be built from the name "SAMUEL."

S—*Softly, in the middle of the night, the Lord delivered His message to a boy,*

A—*And Samuel, because he trusted God, rose to take that message to Eli.*

4. Guide students in developing an outreach acrostic. This poem should be written in class for a specific "outreach" purpose. If students are interested in using an acrostic to help them witness, they might write God's plan of salvation using the motto, "GOD IS LOVE." Consider reproducing copies of the poem for each student. Some may want to promise God they will share their poem and their testimony with at least one non-Christian the coming week.

Or, an adult class might plan an acrostic around a sentence, "WE WILL SAVE YOU A SEAT," and print it in the church bulletin as an invitation to all adults who don't attend Sunday school.

These four ideas all started with the basic acrostic. As you read other suggestions for student writing projects, try to think of at least two creative ways you could use each of them in your class.

Synonymous Parallelism

Even students who have done little creative writing will find developing synonymous parallelisms a successful experience. In this poetic form that is often used in the Bible, the first line states a complete fact, and the second line expresses the same thought through the use

117

of synonyms.

For example, study Isaiah 53: 6.

Line 1—*All we like sheep have gone astray;*
Line 2—*We have turned every one to his own way.*

Or, Psalm 5: 1.

Line 1—*Give ear to my words,*
(O Lord,)
Line 2—*Consider my meditation.*

If a teacher gave his students the line, "I am ashamed before God when I sin," they might write synonymous lines like these:

"I bow my head before my Lord when I do evil in His sight."

"I shrink in sorrow before Christ because I failed Him."

Supply your students with first lines like those, and ask them to write synonymous lines.

1. I will always love my God.
2. It's important for me to do God's will.
3. Christ is both Savior and Lord of my life.

After they have mastered the technique, suggest a topic—the love of God, God's attributes, etc.—and ask students to write original synonymous parallelisms.

Antithetic Parallelism

In antithetic parallelism, the thought is made clear through contrast.

Consider Romans 6: 23.

Line 1—*The wages of sin is death;*
Line 2—*But the gift of God is eternal life.*

Or, Proverbs 10: 1.

Line 1—*A wise son maketh a glad father:*
Line 2—*But a foolish son is the heaviness of his mother.*

Have your students practice writing antithetic lines for the following sentences:

1. When I know that I am in fellowship with God, I am happy.

2. The person who doesn't follow God's way is in for big trouble.

3. When Christians gossip, they ruin their testimonies.

Encourage your students to write original antithetic parallelisms.

WRITING PRAYERS

Most lessons call for a response from the students, and often an immediate and valuable way for them to respond is by writing prayers to God.

When you structure written prayer into your lessons, follow these guidelines:

1. Let students know they will not be asked to share their prayers aloud unless they wish to do so.

2. Suggest they write their prayers using the same language they use when they talk.

3. Challenge them to be honest.

Sometimes teachers encourage dishonesty by assuming everyone in the class is ready to write a prayer to God. Most students will pretend to write something they do not really believe simply to avoid being conspicuous. Always supply an alternate activity. A teacher could ask students to write thank-you notes to God following a lesson on thanksgiving. At the same time, he might suggest those who don't honestly feel thankful and those who don't yet have a prayer relationship with God write the ending to the sentence, "The most important thing I learned from today's lesson is . . . ."

4. Encourage students to pray as specifically as possible.

For example, instead of praying that the Lord bless all the missionaries, a student might bring to Him the requests a missionary made in a prayer letter.

In the following prayer, a seventh-grade boy asked the Lord for help with a specific problem he was having.

119

Dear Lord,
I have this problem.
I can't control my temper.
Yesterday in the basketball game,
I had a technical called on me.
I told the ref off.
Help me, dear Lord. Help me at practice tomorrow.

5. Develop ways in which students' written prayers can continue to be part of their learning experience after they have shared them with God.

Encourage students to take their prayers home with them and read them several times during the week. This will help them remember and follow through on any decisions they made in class.

Usually you will guide your students in writing simple sentences to God explaining how they feel, but occasionally you may want to vary the method. In much the same way as reading a new version of the Bible can help students see new things in a familiar passage, varying the form in which they pray can help them become more aware of what they are saying to God. Adapt the following ideas to your teaching situation, and develop other creative ways to use written prayers in your class hour.

● Suggest students write acrostic prayers or share their thoughts with God through a synonymous parallelism prayer.

● Ask your students to write prayer promises.

Following a lesson on living Christlike lives, one teacher led her teens in writing prayers to God asking Him to help them change problem areas in their personalities. Each student who wished to participate sealed his secret promise in an envelope and put his name on it. Then he made a pact with God to continue to pray and work on the problem for one month. The teacher collected the envelopes. At the end of the month, she returned his unopened envelope to each student. A student's own prayer served as a reminder of his promise and as a help in evaluating how much he had grown.

• Develop a prayer object lesson.

After an adult class had studied a lesson on God's forgiveness, the teacher gave each student an opportunity to write a private prayer confessing a specific sin to God and asking His forgiveness.

Then the teacher said, "If you honestly believe Christ has forgiven your sins, tear your confession into little pieces and throw it away." The prayer served as both a response to God and an object lesson to each student on God's complete forgiveness.

SIMPLE INDUCTIVE BIBLE STUDY

Often students expect their teachers to do their Bible studying for them. Some consider it too much work to dig for themselves, but many who would like to just don't know how. Through simple inductive Bible study, students learn that they can study God's Word for themselves.

Follow these steps:

• Divide the class into study groups of two or three, and supply each person with the same version of the Bible. Bring one dictionary for all groups to refer to. No other resource books should be used.

• Instruct each group to read the portion of Scripture they will be studying three times before students discuss or write anything.

Inductive study takes more time than most in-class creative writing methods, because, to be effective, the students must be given time to become thoroughly involved in the passage. Study sections should be short. If the class were studying salvation, the inductive work might be on John 3: 16-31, or if the topic were Christian brotherhood, the group could study Luke 10: 25-37.

Each group should quickly select a secretary who will record the group's findings and report them to the total class at the end of the study.

• Supply each group with these guidelines to help students structure their study:

1. *What things would you know about (the Bible, sal-*

vation, God, Christ, healing, etc.) *if this were the only section of the Bible you had ever read?*

(To answer this question, ask yourselves: what do the difficult words mean? What relationships are established here? What laws, principles, teachings are stated or implied? Is there an outline? A progression of thought? Repetition of thought or words? What are the key words or phrases? Why? Key verse? What does each verse mean? If necessary, paraphrase.)

2. *What title would you give this section to differentiate it from other sections of Scripture?*

(Be original. Base your title on what you have discovered. Do not simply use the titles which are printed in many Bibles.)

3. *Briefly state how this section applies to us today.*

After students become familiar with inductive study, suggest they begin using the method in their private devotions. Consider making short inductive study homework assignments in which students prepare to share what they have discovered with the class the following week.

SCRIPTURAL CHORAL READING

Guide your students in writing and presenting an original choral reading developed from Scripture.

First, choose a passage which deals with the lesson topic. Usually limit the readings completed in class to only a few verses. You will need a chalkboard or large piece of paper and a student scribe to write what the group suggests.

Make sure each student has a copy of the passage. Ask each one to read it three times. On the first reading, he should try to grasp the general content. On the second reading, he should decide which lines are most important. If possible, he should find what he considers to be the key phrase. On the final reading, he tries to feel the emotion the writer must have felt—for example, sorrow, joy, boldness, fear.

Explain that although they cannot change the words of Scripture, they can vary the order and repeat phrases for emphasis.

Give students an opportunity to decide what key phrase, if any, they will use and with which phrase in the Scripture they will begin.

For example, "Praise to the Lord," might be an excellent key phrase with which to begin and to repeat several times throughout the reading, even though it may appear only once in the psalm the students are scripting.

Now the scribe is ready to begin.

As different members suggest how the phrases and sentences should be arranged in their reading, the scribe records their suggestions on the chalkboard. He should leave a large lefthand margin and double space between each section of copy.

(If time is limited, you may want to complete this much of the choral reading for your students or select a committee to do it. Then reproduce a copy of the reading for each student. As on the chalkboard, double space and allow wide lefthand margins. Even if the total class doesn't become involved until this point, have them read the passage three times, as previously explained.)

After the body has been written, students are ready to assign parts. Explain to them that all the combinations used in singing groups are also possible in a choral reading—male and female choruses, solos, duets, etc. They should let the text help them decide what combinations would be best. If the reading is on the majesty of God, large groups, strong male voices, deliberate female voices should be emphasized. If the passage is on sorrow, solo voices and duets might better capture the mood.

Finally, the students should underline the words they wish speakers to read with special emphasis and mark the volume and, when necessary, the expression they feel would most effectively convey the message.

If a class did a Scriptural choral reading on John 3: 16, 17, it might choose "So loved" as the key phrase and develop a reading something like this one.

JOHN 3: 16, 17

FEMALE SOLO	(*softly*): So loved.
FEMALE DUET	(*gathering strength*): So loved.
ALL:	For God so loved the world, that he gave his only begotten Son,
MALE SOLO:	That whosoever believeth in him should not perish, but have everlasting life.
MALE SOLO:	So loved?
FEMALE SOLO:	Everlasting life?
MALE SOLO	(*emphatically*): So loved.
FEMALE SOLO	(*emphatically*): Everlasting life.
MALE SOLO	(*joyfully*): So loved.
MALE AND FEMALE	(*joyfully*): So loved! Everlasting life!
ALL:	For God sent not his Son into the world to condemn the world;
DUET	(*joyfully*): But that the world through him might be saved.
ALL:	(*loud*): For God so loved.
ALL MALE	(*slightly softer*): So loved the world
FEMALE DUET	(*fading*): So loved.
FEMALE DUET	(*whisper*): So loved.

Students may want to polish an original choral reading and present it to the congregation as part of a church worship service or special holiday program. Suggestions in chapter 2 will help students develop their expression

It is possible for students to become so familiar with a Scripture passage that they grow indifferent to what it is saying.

Perhaps if they rewrite that passage as they think the writer might record it if he lived in their community today, they would rediscover its message.

For example, if the shepherd psalmist of the Old Testament were a contemporary inner-city teen, he might write:

The Lord walks guard beside me; I won't panic.
He keeps me cool like I was under a streetlight.
He leads me down safe alleys.
He turns up the heat and puts glass in the window.
He don't let me do nothing to shame Him.
The Sharks got knives, my friends got needles, but
* I'm clean.*
I got Jesus with me. He never cuts out.
My enemies see me full without busting no heads or
* rolling no dice or stealing no wheels, and I tell them*
* Jesus done it. I got joy.*
The joy will just keep on coming the rest of my days,
* and I got me a pad with Jesus forever.*

Because most students will need at least 15 minutes to prepare their contemporary versions, you may want to make this a homework assignment the week before the familiar passage will be studied in class. Caution the students to thoroughly study the Bible passage before they begin writing so they will be sure to capture the feeling and the message the author intended.

Allow enough class time the following Sunday for all students to share what they have written.

LETTER WRITING

One of the simplest and least used forms of writing in the Sunday school is the letter. Of course, there is often not enough time to complete the letter in class, but if students begin a project they consider worthwhile they will usually complete it on their own at home.

As a service project, a junior high class decided to write to a non-Christian man who was in the hospital dying of cancer. To get them started on the first letter, the teacher wrote suggestions on the chalkboard of things they might include in their letters:

1. A little about your family
2. Something fun you did this week
3. Why you are writing
4. What Christ means to you.

For the first few weeks of the project, the teacher allowed class time for students to get started on their letters. After that she reminded them each Sunday, but each teen assumed his own responsibility for continuing his correspondence outside class.

Every week the junior highs sent new batches of letters to the hospital. In many of them, they shared their simple faith in God.

Dear Mr. Myers,

I don't write many letters because my handwriting isn't so hot. We are having a class party this evening. We're going to put cookies into little bags for children in the hospital. We are also going to put in stories telling of Jesus' love for them.

My parents are Christians, so people expected me to be one too. But I knew I wasn't a Christian just because people believed I was. I thought hard about belonging to Christ. I really am happy that I finally followed Him. I know I will have lots of troubles, but there is always Someone who can help me now.

Jan

The students wrote over 100 letters to Mr. Myers. Not long before he died he wrote back to them that he had become a Christian. "I have found the complete love of Christ, and all my fears have left me," he wrote. "I am a very grateful recipient of your prayers."

The junior highs were amazed at the impact their letters had on the life of this man.

Often the students get as much value from writing their thoughts and expressing how they feel about God as the person who receives the letter.

Consider a project in which your students would write letters to:

• Missionaries or children of missionaries, especially those who are away from their families, attending boarding schools.

• People in homes for senior citizens.

• Shut-ins.

• Servicemen and those at college or away from home for the first time.

• People who don't often get thanked for the work they do in the church (organist, custodian, Sunday school superintendent).

WRITE A SONG

Quite often a class' response to a study of God's Word is one of joy and praise, and what better way to express that feeling than through song! Suggest students write original words to a simple melody with which everyone is familiar.

The class can either work together to write the song or work in small groups to produce many stanzas. The process is simple. Students softly hum the song one line at a time. They brainstorm on possible sentences and phrases that would fit the musical score and finally pick the ones which say best what they want their song to communicate. The class should practice their song several times before they sing it as worship or praise to God.

The following words were written to the melody of "Faith of Our Fathers" and used in an adult class to praise God that He is coming again.

Jesus, my Savior,
I thank You now.
Someday You'll come to earth for me.
O how my happy heart will sing
When You return to earth for me.
Jesus, my Savior,
You will come.
I will be joined with You some day.

Students may want to use their song as the hymn of the month and sing it each Sunday. If they wrote original words to one song a month, they could compile their songs into a class hymnal at the end of the year.

FINISH THE STORY

Introduce creative story writing to your class by setting up "what if" situations for them to complete. Use some of the ideas suggested below or develop your own. Allow about ten minutes for this activity.

1. What if the little girl Christ raised from the dead had kept a diary? Write what you think her entry might have been on the day after He healed her.

2. What if you had been one of the people visiting Jerusalem on the day of Christ's crucifixion? You had never heard of Jesus before, but out of curiosity you followed Him to Calvary and watched Him die. Write a letter to your friends back home telling them what you saw and how you felt about it.

3. What if you were a Roman newspaper man who had been given an opportunity to interview Paul during his house arrest in Rome? Write the first few paragraphs of that story. Include what you learned about him and how you felt about what he said.

Often students can finish a story as a homework assignment. Homework story-starters can be more involved than "what if" situations done in class. It is ideal if each student can have a copy of the story starter to take home with him.

The following example would make an excellent homework assignment for students to bring to class Easter Sunday morning.

ON GUARD

What if you were one of the Roman guards assigned to guard Jesus' tomb? While you were on duty, there was an earthquake. Someone dressed in white clothing —with an appearance like lightning—rolled the stone away from the tomb's door. The Roman seal was broken! You were so afraid that you and the other guards became like dead men.

Later the high priest paid you money and said, "You will tell people His disciples came while you were sleeping. They stole the body."

You were frightened and did what you were told. But years have passed, and now you are faced with another decision concerning Jesus.

Julius paced the floor of the barracks.

"Settle down," his friend Marcus advised. "What are your new orders? How could they possibly upset you this much?"

"I've been ordered to round up Christians because they are enemies of the state."

"And good lion food," Marcus laughed. "That's not so bad. You've had worse assignments than this. Weren't you a guard over their Leader's tomb?"

"I wish I'd never heard of Jesus," Julius said. "Marcus, I'm going to tell you a story that could make lion food out of me. Then I'm going to ask you what you would do about these orders."

He turned to his friend and said, ". . .

FINISH THIS STARTER

BIBLE REVIEW NEWSPAPER
(*Young Teen Activity*)
After your students have completed a large unit of

129

study, perhaps on the life of Christ or the Patriarchs, plan a Bible newspaper competition to help them review.

Divide the class into two or more newspaper staffs. Explain that each staff will be competing against the others to give the most complete and interesting newspaper coverage of the events they have just studied.

Explain that their papers will be judged by the following criteria:

• *Originality of their newspaper's name—5 points.* For example, "The Patriarchal Times," or "The Galilee Gazette."

• *Coverage of the material studied—25 points.* Students should write their news articles as though the events just happened. Reporting should be interesting and factual.

• *Lessons we have learned from this material and how we can use them in our lives—30 points.* This is the editorial section in which teens share how this study has affected their lives. These articles should be written in the first person. It may include titles such as "The Verse That Meant the Most to Me," "What I Learned from the Life of —————," "A Decision I Have Made."

• *Use of visuals (maps, pictures, charts)—10 points.*

• *Creative features—10 points.* This may include things like original crossword puzzles and cartoons. In a review newspaper on the Israelites' journey from Egypt to Canaan, one reporter included a humorous recipe for camel stew.

• *Choice of lead story—10 points.* This is the story which the staff agrees was the most meaningful and important one of the unit for them. The reasons for their choice should be included in the lead story.

• *Headlines used—10 points.*

• *Neatness—5 points.*

Show the students the size of the newspaper. Consider using large sheets of wrapping paper, approximately 20 x 28 inches. Explain that they should plan to use only one side of the paper. (This will make the papers easier to post so students can read each other's work.)

Allow about half a period for students to get organized. In this time, they should choose an editor and decide what articles they will need. The editor will assign at least one homework article to each student. It is also the editor's responsibility to make sure everyone on his staff completes his assignments. The editor should encourage his staff to write their homework as neatly as possible since their articles will be pasted directly on the newspaper.

Devote the entire next Sunday to putting the papers together and discussing them. In addition to a large sheet of paper, each group will need paste, scissors, and felt marker for writing the newspaper's name.

Either you, a group of students, or someone from outside the class should judge the newspapers and explain the reason why the first-place winner was chosen.

After the newspapers have been completed, lead the class in discussion. Use questions like these:

In what ways was the study of _____ valuable to you?

How have you been able to use what you have learned?

What new things did you learn during the newspaper review?

If you could share just one article in your newspaper with a non-Christian teen, which one would it be? Why?

If your teens enjoyed the newspaper project, they may want to start a monthly class news letter. Perhaps one staff could be responsible for the letter one month and another staff the next. The paper could include things such as:

• Excerpts (25 lines or less) from missionary letters.

• Short message (25 lines or less) from the class president or teacher.

• List of coming events.

• Hello interview—interview with one member of the

class each month to help the rest of the class get to know him or her better.

- Samples of creative things students have done in class (original songs, poems, etc.).
- Features about special projects the class is involved in.

WRITING PARABLES
(*Homework Activity*)

Many teens and adults are capable of writing meaningful, original parables.

Begin by making sure students understand what a parable is—a short, simple story from which a lesson may be drawn. Read together some of Jesus' parables and discuss how He used them to teach His followers. Then to give your students examples of contemporary parables, read and discuss "Marvin" and "A Modern Christian at the Well."

MARVIN
(This parable was written by an eighth-grade student, Dawn Berg.)

One day while riding across a large cattle range, Ben found Marvin, a small turtle who was starving because he was blind and unable to find food. Ben found Marvin, so Marvin belonged to him.

It was Ben's job to supply the turtle's needs by directing him toward things that would be good for him. For instance, day after day, Ben would place Marvin's food where he could locate it by his sense of smell. Sometimes Marvin succeeded, but other times he would ignore his sense of smell and go astray.

One day Marvin got tired of being under Ben's direction. "I can get along fine without Ben," he thought. He didn't realize that as he walked away, Ben continued to watch him.

All morning Marvin walked. "I've come a great way without Ben," he thought proudly. But Ben could see he had been walking in circles.

132

As time passed and Marvin got hungry, his pride began to waver. The air got cooler, and Marvin could tell it would soon be night. Finally he admitted his mistake. "Help, Ben!" he called.

Ben's voice came from very near him. "Right over here!" And when Marvin returned, he found Ben had kept his supper there waiting for him.

"I'm sorry, Ben," Marvin said. "Thank you."

Discussion:

• Who do you think Ben and Marvin represent in this parable?

• State in a single sentence what this parable is teaching?

• What are some ways God uses to bring Christians back to Him when they act like Marvin did?

A MODERN CHRISTIAN AT THE WELL

Then cometh Christian from out the suburbs into the inner city. Now the slums were there. It was about three o'clock, and Christian had been handing out tracts, proclaiming the Lord, witnessing hither and yon for many hours, and his thirst was great.

"Would you mind telling me whence you purchased that cola?" he asked of a young woman.

"Not for nearly six blocks would you find such a thing," she answered. Looking at the weary Christian and his sweaty tracts, she smiled and held out the remaining inch in the bottle.

Leery of germs and communicable diseases, he drew back. This woman had a slight odor not at all pleasant or acceptable in Christian circles, and under the afternoon sun, she had gird about her simply a robe.

"I have come to offer you living water," he diverted her. "Whosoever drinketh of this water shall never thirst again."

The woman saith unto him, "Sir, how is it that one dressed so properly comes to minister to me?"

"It is love for your soul which has brought me into

this dreary, dismal place." And uttering a dry, thirsty cough, he handed her a tract.

The woman saith, "I am most interested in this water. Enter into my abode, and we shall discuss further."

Noting the locality and the condition of the building, Christian thought of what people would think if they saw him go in with a woman. "Yes, let's talk, but here on the doorstep."

So in the scorching sun, they stood.

A tiny child tottered from out the highrise, and Christian looked down and smiled paternally. The child reached its arms to be lifted up, but Christian noted the hanging diaper and the heavy chest rash. Reaching deep into his pocket, he put into the child's hand a shining dime. The child looked at the dime and at Christian, then toddled over to his mother.

Christian subtly asked of the child's father and thus brought into the open the total depravity. With much flourish and the thought of many stars in his crown, Christian preached Christ, forgiveness, salvation through love.

And upon this came up the street a member of his Sunday school class who bestowed such a look on the man and his projected convert that Christian reddened to his Adam's apple.

"Tell me more of this love He offers," said the woman, wondering at Christian's discomposure.

"Yes, yes. I will come back on a morrow." As Christian hastened toward his friend to begin the tale of blessings he had received on his day of witnessing, the woman did watch and wonder.

And the woman told many of her friends about her Christian visitor, and they would shake their heads as they walked away.

● Put the message of this parable into a single sentence. Why is this message of great importance to the Christian church today?

• In what practical ways can we witness to those around us? To those who live in areas where there is very little Christian influence?

PARABLE-STARTERS

Choose one of these parable-starters that deals with a subject you will be teaching, and ask students to develop it as a homework assignment. The Sunday the assignment is due, give opportunity for each student to share what he has written and for the class to discuss the message found in each parable.

Encourage students who have ability in this area to continue writing original parables. Consider compiling their creative work into a class booklet of parables.

1. *Aim: to help students grasp how important it is to follow God.*

A young Canadian goose refuses to follow the leader and decides that instead of flying south, he will stay in northern Canada for the winter. Write what happens to the foolish goose and how he learns that even though it involves work to follow the leader, it is also very important.

2. *Aim: to help students understand that in order for God's Church to move forward, each Christian must do his share.*

Write about a lazy team horse who comes into a farmyard. He pulls only half his share of a load and often plays sick. Tell how the actions of the horse affect life in the barnyard. Include how the farmer eventually deals with the problem.

3. *Aim: to help students recognize how important it is to keep witnessing even when there seem to be no positive results.*

Write about a garden in which all the plants are drooping, except one. That one has discovered that if she lifts her leaves up, she catches the sun, and if she digs her roots down, she finds water. These discoveries are saving her life. Write what happens when she tries to share what she has found with the other plants.

1. EXCHANGE PRAYERS. Each student writes and then exchanges an important prayer request with another person. The two promise each other that every day for the next week they will remember to pray for their exchange requests.

2. SHARING BOX. Place a box in the classroom and invite students to put into it questions, problems, and comments which they would like to share with you. These may be either signed or unsigned.

3. GRAFFITI WALL for teens. Cover one wall or section of a wall with wrapping paper, and invite students to write their comments about a specific topic (God's love, God's presence, being a Christian, etc.) on it. Encourage them to record original slogans, Bible verses, relevant thoughts. A graffiti wall makes an excellent pre- and post-class activity.

4. KEY VERSE. Give the students time to copy a key verse from the lesson onto a 3 x 5-inch card. Suggest they place the card where they will see it every day and be reminded of the truth it contains.

5. PROVERBS AND MOTTOES. Have students restate the lessons they have learned in the form of proverbs or mottoes. For example, after a lesson on Christian conduct, a student might write "God specializes in helping me pass life's tests" (proverb) or "My Christian Goal— Zero Defects!" (motto).

Teen students may enjoy making posters or car and bike bumper stickers from their creations.

6. SPIRITUAL GEOGRAPHY. Post a large map of the world, country, or area where you live, and supply each student with little paper flags and straight pins. Ask them to write their names on their flags and pin them on the map at the places where important events in their

spiritual lives took place. Give opportunity for students to share what happened at certain "flags" if they wish to do so.

7. HUMOROUS COUPLETS AND LIMERICKS. Suggest students write humorous rhyming couplets or limericks to emphasize an important point in the lesson. For example:

Wearing clothes all squeaky and new
Doesn't make God impressed with you.
   Or,
A fine Christian man once said, "Hey,
Our country's going the wrong way.
Of course, I don't vote!"
He cleared his deep throat,
"Instead, I sit home and pray."

8. CHAIN REACTION STORY. Give each student a piece of paper, and ask him to write an ending to the sentence you will give. Then he should fold his answer back so no one else can see it and pass his paper to the person on his right. This person will finish the second sentence you give, fold his answer under, and pass the paper to his right. This process continues until the story is finished. Then each person unfolds the story he is holding and reads it to the class.

For example, if the lesson were on the problems of living for Christ in a secular school situation, a chain reaction story might be built around finishing the following sentences:

- Joel became a Christian because . . .

- The biggest problem he will face in his Christian life at school will be _____, because . . .

- One way Joel can get help with problems in his Christian life is by . . .

- Joel asks you what you think the secret to a successful Christian life is, and you say . . .

7

ART PROJECTS

Lessons your students can make...

In one corner of the classroom, several students were studying a Bible atlas. Other groups were making lists of materials, drawing diagrams, discussing who in the congregation might be resource people. They were preparing to build a model of the city of Jerusalem in Christ's day.

Just one week before, the class had sat silent, polite, disinterested, uninvolved with the lesson or each other.

Miss Root, their teacher, was determined to unite the class and get them excited about the Bible as a living Book. Easter was just a few Sundays away when she had an idea. She was teaching the life of Christ. Why not have the students reconstruct the city of Jerusalem, Calvary, and the garden tomb as part of the Bible study, and display what they make to the whole church on Easter morning? However, she knew that to be worthwhile, the building of the city had to be more than an exciting activity. Of what real value was the project?

A successful project must blend with the lesson aim and be part of the ongoing teaching process. To help her evaluate her idea, Miss Root made a list of the benefits her students would receive from making the city:

- will become involved in inductive Bible study
- will learn to use reference material
- will learn to work together as a unit
- will remember the events in the last week of Jesus' life and the significance of those events more vividly after building a three-dimensional model

138

• will have to decide what their relationship to Christ is, based on accompanying Bible study and discussion

• will give them a sense of satisfaction to complete a project and display it for the entire church

• will serve as catalyst (possibly) to get families who don't attend church to come see what their teens made.

Her list left no doubt as to the project's value to her class.

Many different projects are suggested in this chapter. Evaluate each one's worth to your students before you incorporate it into your lesson. The following questions will help you guide your evaluation.

1. Can you adapt the project to the age level and capabilities of your students?

2. Does the project fit your lesson's aim so students will be learning as well as participating? Does the project give them an opportunity to grow spiritually?

3. Does what the students will learn justify the amount of time the project will take?

4. Will the project hold the students' attention? It is unrealistic to always expect 100 percent participation, but aim for the highest possible student involvement. By using a variety of teaching methods, you can boost student interest—for example, complete an art project one quarter, write original songs the next, and perhaps develop and present a mime drama the following quarter.

5. Have you prayed about the project and the students who will be involved in it?

Projects should never be busywork. They are important tools teachers can use to introduce and involve students in the Christian life and to help them better understand how they can work for God as members of His family.

TANGRAM ART

A tangram is a square of any size that has been cut into seven pieces in this way:

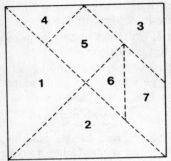

These pieces can be arranged to form many different designs.

Cut the tangrams before class and place each in an envelope. If possible, use colorful construction paper, although any type of paper can be used. Size will vary according to the size of the background piece of paper on which each student will arrange his tangram. For example a 3½-inch square would fit nicely on a 9 x 12 background sheet.

A tangram project can be an extremely effective teaching aid. First, it equalizes students by giving them all the same seven pieces with which to work. Each student may use his pieces to either create a realistic picture or to symbolically represent what he wants to communicate. Second, it forces the student to think through what he has learned, and how he can best illustrate this so others will also learn. And finally, he explains his picture to his classmates. Through this, he gains experience sharing with others about his God and his Christian faith.

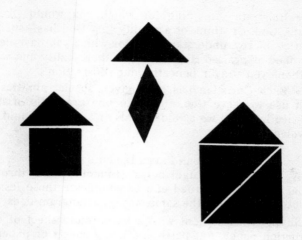

This tangram was created by an eighth-grade boy. He explained it to the rest of the students by saying, "My picture shows a church on the left and a home on the right. That's me in the center. Because my parents are Christians, I learn about God at both places."

The first time you use tangrams in class, explain what a tangram is and show an example which you have created. It should take about five minutes for students to arrange their pieces and tape or paste them on their background sheets. Allow enough time after the tangrams are finished for each person to explain his creation. Consider using one of the following assignments or developing an original tangram activity.

• Illustrate something you would like to tell the world about Christ's love.

• What story in the Bible means the most to you right now? Illustrate it with your tangram and be ready to share your story and the reason for your choice with the class.

• Use your tangram to explain to a non-Christian one important thing about God's plan for man's salvation.

• Illustrate something for which you would like to thank God. Or, think of a quality that God has—such as justice, mercy, understanding—for which you have never thanked or praised Him. Illustrate that quality and write a thank-you prayer beneath your illustration.

• Each Christian has been given special abilities he can use to serve God. Illustrate one area of Christian service in which we as individuals or as a class could get involved.

TORN-PAPER DESIGNS

A torn-paper design helps students think through what they have learned and communicate those lessons to others, in much the same way as a tangram does.

Supply each student with a background sheet of construction paper. Put paste and many sheets of paper to be torn within easy reach of all students. (No scissors should be used.) Ask them to tear and paste a design on the background and be ready to explain their finished pictures. Explain that the finished design may be either realistic or symbolic.

Allow about ten minutes for the creation of the pictures and enough time for each student to explain what he has created. If it fits your lesson aim, use an assignment suggestion from the tangram section of this chapter, or develop an assignment of your own.

WATER COLOR, AN INDUCTIVE BIBLE STUDY

Choose a short Scripture passage dealing with your lesson's subject, and ask students to read it to themselves at least three times. Suggest they ask themselves as they are reading, "What does this section of God's Word say to me? What might the writer have been feeling as he wrote these verses? What do I feel—love, joy, awe, sorrow, anticipation?"

Supply a box of dime store watercolors for every four students, and a sheet of paper and a brush for each. After they have read the passage, ask students to work in complete silence as they try to capture with color and lines, rather than with a realistic drawing, the feeling of this verse. Plan on about 15 minutes for the reading and the watercolor.

Allow time for each student to explain his watercolor. Students may want to conclude this project by writing sentence prayers on their creations.

You can vary the basic water color project. For example, place a number of references dealing with the morning's topic in a box, and have students choose one at random to study, paint, and explain to the rest of the class.

Or, assign each verse of the study section to a different student. A student would read the entire section, but illustrate only the feeling he finds in his verse. For example, if the class were studying Psalm 100, a student illustrating verse 1 might paint a green circle in the center of his picture to represent the world. Coming from that circle could be wide orange brushstrokes which indicate the feeling of joy all the world should have because the Lord rules.

COLOR BLOCKS

Cut a number of different colored three-inch squares before class. Then during the lesson ask students to each choose a square in a color that represents something to them. For example:

1. Choose the color that you think best represents the successful Christian life.

2. Choose the color that you think best represents Christmas (or any Christian holiday) to a non-Christian. Then choose the color that represents the meaning of Christmas to you.

3. Choose a color that you could use to tell the world's people something important you think they should know about God.

Give opportunity for each student to share why he chose the color he did. Often it is also valuable to have students write something on their blocks which will remind them of the lesson the block helped teach. With the above examples, a student might write:

1. A promise to God that you will work to improve one specific problem area in your Christian life.

2. A prayer to God thanking Him for the event the holiday is commemorating and asking Him for opportunities to share that holiday's true message with others.

3. The name of one non-Christian you will speak to about Christ this coming week.

WOODBLOCK BOOK
(Teen Class Project Involving Homework)

Plan a woodblock book on a subject such as the life of a Bible character, the story of salvation, the Biblical rules for living a Christian life.

Divide the class into working pairs. Each pair will be responsible for one page in the book. A page will contain copy explaining one part of the book's message and one woodblock print.

In class, students should decide what copy will be covered on each page of the book. Ideally they should be given time, about 15 minutes, to write their pages' message. If this is not realistic, ask them to bring their finished assignment to class the following Sunday. Type or have one member of each pair copy what they have written onto a stencil. Use no more than half a page for copy since the other half will be needed for the woodblock. Reproduce enough pages so each student will get two copies of the entire book.

After the copy is completed have the pairs discuss what woodblock picture could illustrate what they have written. Students may want to sketch a few ideas and get their classmates' opinions of them. Suggest they use large shapes in their design since these reproduce better than small, intricate ones. Then plan a time outside class when the group can get together to cut the blocks and print them on their pages. Each pair should print two copies of its woodblock for every student in the class.

A number of different printing methods can be used.

A. Students should cut a large potato in half. They can transfer their paper sketch onto the potato by cutting out the sketch, holding it on the flat, cut surface of the potato, and lightly tracing around it with a toothpick or other sharp instrument. Then they should carve away everything except the design they wish to print. When it is completed, they should spread printing (fast-drying) ink over the raised surface and press it carefully onto the paper.

B. Students should trace their design on cardboard, cut it out, and paste it on another piece of cardboard or plywood. Printing ink should be spread on the raised surface and the design pressed carefully onto the paper.

C. Excellent prints can be made by cutting linoleum blocks, if special cutting tools are available. This woodblock was done by a seventh-grade class member as part of a review of the life of David.

After the books are assembled, students should discuss what they learned from working together and about the subject covered in their books.

Suggest each of them keep one book and give the other to someone he would like to interest in coming to Sunday school.

MOBILES
(Teen Homework or Class Party Project)

Consider the following ways mobiles might be used in the teaching process.

• As a review, print the references of Bible verses your students have studied this quarter on small slips of paper. Put them in a box, and have each student draw one at random. Then give each a piece of cardboard or heavy construction paper. Explain that as a homework assignment, he is to find a picture which he feels illustrates or captures the mood of his verse, and paste that picture on one side of the cardboard. On the other side, he should write his verse or an important phrase from it.

On the Sunday the assignments are due, take about ten minutes at the beginning of the period to assemble the mobile, hang it in the room, and talk about the verses included on it. You might include questions like this in your discussion:

1. In what way does your picture illustrate your verse?

2. If you could share just one of these verses with a non-Christian friend, which would you pick? Why?

3. Which of the verses on our mobile means to most to you today? Why?

• Use a mobile homework assignment to illustrate a specific lesson. For example, if next Sunday's lesson were on integrity, you could ask each student to find a newspaper picture in which people are showing a lack of integrity. He should paste that picture on a piece of cardboard or construction paper you will give him, and on the other side write how that picture might have been different if the people involved had shown integrity.

In class, have the students show their pictures, read what they have written, and assemble the mobile. This activity could lead into a Bible study of what God says about integrity.

Or, if the lesson were on God's love, each student could paste a picture of how God has shown His love through nature on one side of the cardboard. On the other he could write a verse on God's love which he found by using a Bible concordance.

• Plan a mobile party as a service project. Make mobiles for sick children, shut-ins, or senior citizens. Ask students to bring pictures to use on the mobiles. Suggest they choose a motto for each mobile that might meet the need of the person receiving it. For example, "We're Praying for You," or "Jesus Loves and Cares for You." This motto should be written on two or more of the mobile parts.

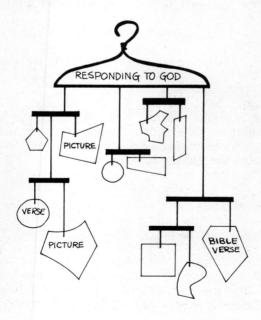

To make a mobile:

1. Paste pictures on cardboard or construction paper. Cut construction paper into odd sizes. Write the verse, motto, etc., on the other side of the cardboard.

2. Use a clothes hanger, pole, or stick as your mobile base.

If you use the hanger, you may want to cover it with paper, and write the verse or motto on the paper (see illustration). Tape the sides of this paper around the hanger, but leave the bottom of the hanger open so you can tie strings to it.

3. Tie several strings of different lengths to the base. Tie plastic straws that have been cut to different sizes or sticks to the ends of the strings. Sew a thread through each picture, and tie a picture to each end of the straw. Balance each straw by moving the threads back and forth. Mobiles with from ten to twelve pieces usually work best, although students may enjoy developing more complex ones.

4. Use string or ribbon to hang the mobile from the ceiling.

Students can vary the mobile project by making paper sculptures. As with the mobile, copy and pictures are backed with cardboard.

A simple base can be built from two identical rectangles. Students slit one vertically from the bottom-center to the middle of the rectangle. They slit the other vertically from the top-center to the middle. Then the two pieces will slip together and stand.

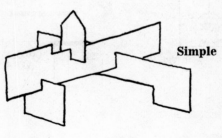

Simple

Students can add other pieces to their sculpture by slitting each piece and fitting it over another. A finished sculpture may look like one of these.

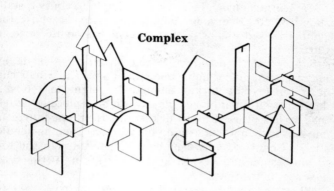

Complex

SYMBOLS
(*Using symbols in diagrams*)

Often high school and adult lessons deal with concepts. Suggest students draw a diagram illustrating a concept with the use of lines, symbols, and perhaps a few words. Students will learn both from organizing their thoughts into diagrams and from explaining what they have drawn to their classmates. Their diagrams could also alert you to any misunderstandings they may have.

Consider how your students might diagram:
• Christ as mediator between God and man
• The Holy Spirit's function in the lives of Christians today
• Christ's plan for the end of the age

Have each student draw with a crayon rather than a pencil. His diagram will tend to be freer and others in the class will have less difficulty seeing it.

SYMBOL PARTY
(*Teen Project*)

Following a study on the symbols of the Christian

church or as a special holiday activity, plan a symbol party with your students. Ask each to come to the party with at least one symbol pattern he has drawn—cross, Dove, Ichthus (fish), bell, circle, triangle (Trinity), staff, star, lily, etc. Everyone should share why he chose the symbol he did and why that symbol has significance to Christians.

Supply each student with dough you have made by mixing four cups of flour, one cup of salt, and a half cup of water (recipe makes enough for eight to ten students). Each should place his pattern on a piece of dough that he has pressed to a thickness of from one-fourth to one-half inch, and cut around his pattern. Then he should stick a Christmas tree ornament holder through the top of his design, and bake it at 350 degrees until the symbols are light brown.

When the dough has cooled, a student may want to paint his symbol.

Students could use symbols to decorate a Christmas tree. Or, they could decorate an Easter branch with symbols of Christ's resurrection. Symbols could also be hung from the ceiling on strings of various lengths to form a meaningful and unusual room decoration any time of the year.

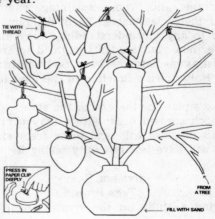

TIE WITH THREAD

PRESS IN PAPER CLIP DEEPLY

FROM A TREE

FILL WITH SAND

COLLAGE AND MONTAGE

A collage is a picture that has been made by arranging flat objects—such as newspaper, cloth, pressed flowers—on a background sheet in such a way that the objects emphasize a theme or have a symbolic meaning. In a montage, the pieces included in the picture may be three-dimensional. They are arranged so they form a single picture without losing their individual distinctiveness. For example, a teen might do a service montage. The background could be composed of pieces of colored cellophane representing a church stained-glass window. On this could be arranged items which represent services teens can render to the church—dust ball (cleaning), coins (giving), old watch (time).

Assign montage and collage projects to be completed as homework and displayed and discussed in class. Or, ask students to bring to class what they will need to develop a design on a specific topic. They should not use class time to collect materials.

Assign one of the following collage-montage ideas to your students or develop an original assignment around a lesson you will be teaching.

• GET-ACQUAINTED COLLAGE OR MONTAGE. In a large class where people have difficulty getting to know each other, or following a promotion Sunday, ask each student to make a small collage or montage using pictures or items that he thinks would help others learn important things about him. For example, a man might use pictures of cars (he's a car salesman), a golf tee (hobby), and pictures of fancy desserts (enjoys gourmet cooking).

In class each student could explain his picture and in this way introduce himself to the group.

Or, you could collect all the pictures before the students show them to each other, display them, and have students guess who did each picture.

This project helps students become better acquainted so they will feel more comfortable sharing spiritual things with each other and growing together through the Sunday school year.

• STORY-OF-SALVATION COLLAGE. Ask students to bring to class newspaper or magazine clippings that illustrate man's sin. Hang a large sheet of paper on the wall and label it "Man's Sin." Have students paste their pictures on this sheet. Pictures may be cut in unusual sizes, overlap, or be placed helter-skelter on the collage.

Then, following a Bible study on God's solution for man's sin, give each student a small piece of paper on which you have written the title, "God's Solution." Ask him to write in his own words God's message of salvation, and then tape his solution over the pictures on the sheet. The finished collage will look something like this:

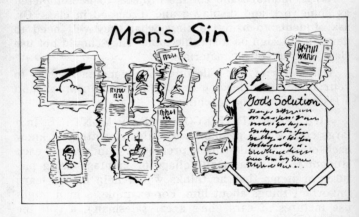

• ECOLOGY MONTAGE. In preparation for a lesson on the Christian's responsibility to the world God has entrusted to his care, give each student a double assignment. Ask him to bring to class pictures showing the beauty of nature and also one piece of litter he has picked up.

In class each student should tape his nature picture to one side of the montage and his trash to the other. Following the Bible study, give each student a 3 x 5 card, and ask him to write a prayer to God stating one specific thing he will do to make the world a better place in which to live. Post these cards around the montage.

This activity can lead your students into a discussion about projects through which they could help fight pollution. For example, teens may want to have a paper and glass drive. Adults may decide to boycott products which pollute or waste our natural resources, or write editorials against industries that break anti-pollution laws.

PHOTOGRAPHY

In nearly every class there are students who enjoy photography. Involve these students in photographic projects that will increase the impact of the lesson on the whole class and give those students opportunities to use their abilities to serve Christ.

PRAYER CARDS

Following a lesson on prayer, suggest students make prayer cards to remind themselves to pray for church missionaries, church leaders, sick people, students and servicemen away from home, etc. The photographer should take a picture of the person or people the class decides to especially remember in prayer and have a copy reproduced for each student.

Prayer cards can be made from construction paper that has been cut to approximately 4½ x 9 inches and folded in half. On one side students should mount the picture and write the person's name, address, and phone number. On the other side, they should write specific prayer requests for this person. As they pray, students should record God's answers on the inside of their cards.

This idea could be expanded into an all-church project if students made cards available to anyone who would promise to pray for the person on his card.

SCRIPTURE LESSON WITH SLIDES

About six weeks before you want to use a Scripture and slide presentation, select a committee to study your lesson's Bible text. Ask them to work with a class photographer to find ways to illustrate the mood and message of the verses. After the pictures are taken and processed, the photographer and a reader from the committee should work together to coordinate the Scripture reading with the pictures.

Consider how a slide presentation might make a familiar passage like Ephesians 6: 10-13 come alive to students.

Verse 10
1. Mountain
2. Large tree
3. Person sitting alone on ground with back to camera

Be strong in the Lord, and in the power of His might.

Verse 11
4—6. Crowd scenes

Put on the complete armor that God supplies, so you will be able to stand against the devil's intrigues.

Verse 12	*For our wrestling is not*
7—8. Out-of-focus crowd scenes	*against flesh-and-blood opponents, but against rulers,*
9—10. Out-of-focus blurs of people's faces	*the authorities, the cosmic powers of this present darkness, against the spiritual forces of evil in heavenly spheres.*
Verse 13	*Take up, therefore, the*
11. Grass blowing in wind	*whole armor of God so that you may be able to stand*
12. Tree blowing in wind	*when you have done all the fighting.*
13. Person from shot 3, standing, back to camera, arms outstretched, feet apart, expressing joy, victory	

After students have successfully used this method in class, they may want to share what they have done with others. Suggest they build a slide presentation around the pastor's sermon Scripture and show it during the morning worship hour.

Or, encourage them to plan an original Christmas or Easter program in which they use Scripture and slides to share God's message with others.

REACH OUT
with
additional
copies
of
this
book...

Simply ask for them at your local bookstore—or order from the David C. Cook Publishing Co., Elgin, IL 60120 (in Canada: Weston, Ont. M9L 1T4).

If you've just finished this book, we think you'll agree . . .

A COOK PAPERBACK IS

REWARDING READING

Try some more!

HOW SILENTLY, HOW SILENTLY by Joseph Bayly. Fantastic entertainment . . . with meaning YOU decide! Thirteen tales of mystery, drama, humor, science fiction lead to discovery.
73304—$1.25

FAITH AT THE TOP by Wesley Pippert. From a seasoned Washington reporter . . . a look at 10 eminently successful people who dared to bring Christ with them all the way.
75796—$1.50

LOOK AT ME, PLEASE LOOK AT ME by Clark, Dahl and Gonzenbach. Accepting the retarded—with love—as told in the moving struggle of two women who learned how.
72595—$1.25

THE 13TH AMERICAN by Pastor Paul. Every 13th American is an alcoholic, and it could be anyone. A sensitive treatment of alcoholism by a minister who fought his way back.
72629—$1.50

THE EVIDENCE THAT CONVICTED AIDA SKRIPNIKOVA edited by Bourdeaux and Howard-Johnston. Religious persecution in Russia! The story of a young woman's courage.
72652—$1.25

LET'S SUCCEED WITH OUR TEENAGERS by Jay Kesler. Substitutes hope for parental despair—offers new understanding that exposes the roots of parent-child differences.
72660—$1.25

THE PROPHET OF WHEAT STREET by James English. Meet William Borders, a Southern Black educated at Northwestern University, who returned to lead the black church in Atlanta.
72678—$1.25

WHAT A WAY TO GO! by Bob Laurent. Your faith BEYOND church walls. Laurent says, "Christianity is not a religion, it's a relationship." Freedom, new life replace dull routine!
72728—$1.25

THE VIEW FROM A HEARSE (new enlarged edition) by Joseph Bayly. Examines suicide. Death can't be ignored—what is the Christian response? Hope is as real as death.
73270—$1.25

WHAT'S SO GREAT ABOUT THE BIBLE (new enlarged edition) by James Hefley. Hefley presents the Bible as a literary miracle, an indestructible influence in the world.

73288—$1.25

WHAT ABOUT HOROSCOPES? by Joseph Bayly. A topic on everyone's mind! As the author answers the question posed by the title, he also discusses witches, other occult subjects.

51490—95¢

IS THERE HEALING POWER? by Karl Roebling. A keen interest in healing led the author to a quest of facts. A searching look at faith healers: Kathryn Kuhlman, Oral Roberts, others.

68460—95¢

HOW TO ENJOY THE GOD STUFF by Hugh Claycombe. All cartoons, it's a fresh, funny/serious look at our goals, values, relationships . . . as they seem to us, and as Jesus sees them.

75838—$1.25

THE KENNEDY EXPLOSION by E. Russell Chandler. An exciting new method of lay evangelism boosts a tiny Florida church from 17 to 2,450 members. Over 50,000 copies sold.

63610—95¢

STRANGE THINGS ARE HAPPENING by Roger Ellwood. Takes you for a close look at what's happening in the world of Satanism and the occult today . . . and tells what it means.

68478—95¢

Order books from your local bookstore . . . or David C. Cook Publishing Co., Elgin, IL 60120 (in Canada: Weston, Ont. M9L 1T4), *using coupon below.*

Name _____

Address _____

City _____ State _____ ZIP Code _____

TITLE	STOCK NO.	PRICE	QTY.	ITEM TOTAL
		$		$
			Subtotal	$

NOTE: On orders placed with David C. Cook Publishing Co., add handling charge of 25¢ for first dollar, plus 5¢ for each additional dollar.

Handling _____

TOTAL $ _____